The Food for Life Cookbook

To Mum's burnt peas
and all our ZOE members

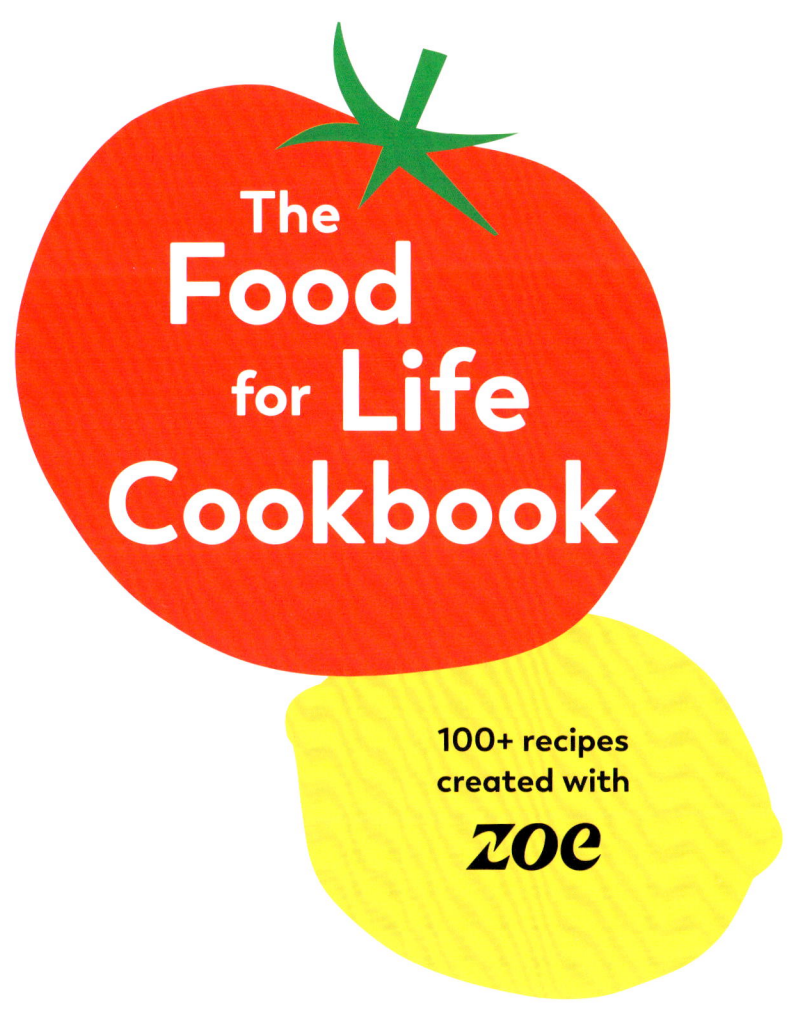

TIM SPECTOR

Recipes by Kathryn Bruton and Georgia Tyler
with Dr. Federica Amati

TEN SPEED PRESS
California | New York

Contents

6 Introduction

    My Journey to Food for Life

    Back to Basics: The Six Principles of Food for Life

    How to Use This Book

62 Everyday Essentials

74 Mornings

98 15-Minute Meals

124 Vibrant Salads

150 Satisfying Mains

176 Pantry Raid

198 Entertaining

218 Sweet Treats

242 Snacks

260 Score Boosters

272 Index

284 Acknowledgments

My Journey to Food for Life

Food for me is the perfect combination of science and pleasure; the more I learn, the better it tastes. When you discover the amazing complexity of what's going on in your body every single time you take a bite—and all the trillions of microorganisms that depend on what you eat—it's quite humbling. Your food choices are simply the most important ones you can make for your overall health and happiness.

While I can tap into this knowledge now, it's still only relatively recently that we've been able to connect the dots between the science of food, the art of cooking, and their interactions with our health. With this cookbook, I want to share my knowledge with you and show you how simple it can be to eat for both pleasure *and* health. The recipes build from the six key principles for eating well that I set out in my book *Food for Life*. In those pages, I examined the latest science and made the case for changing the way we eat in theory; this book is all about turning that theory into practice. Working with brilliant chefs and nutritionists from ZOE, the science and nutrition company that I co-founded, we've created recipes that will help you adopt and live these six principles in your own life to help you make better food choices every day, whatever your starting point.

So, let's start at the beginning. I was brought up with an appreciation of the pleasure of food, but as in most families, it was mainly considered as fuel, with just a few specific benefits: fish made you brainy, meat made you strong, and spinach gave you iron and muscles. It may come as a surprise, but I was not raised in a gourmet household. My mother, June, is a very down-to-earth Australian (Juno to her Aussie friends), and when my brother and I were kids, she had a fairly narrow culinary repertoire. We were lucky to have a lovely vegetable plot and apple trees, and everything was served simply, usually without any sauces or herbs and spices (except garlic). She could do the basics, so we had a lot of fried foods and meat and two vegetables, but fish was pretty rare. Because she was brought up in the war years, she would eat absolutely anything. When we traveled abroad, she would seek out the most weird and wonderful foods; I can remember being transfixed as I watched her eat whole baby squid, lungs, sweetbreads, and brains. In light of her culinary curiosity, my brother and I became accustomed to trying a diverse range of foods too.

Since my mum worked as a part-time physiotherapist, and the only thing my dad ever made was sandwiches on Sunday,

I was taught to cook for myself from a young age, though that usually meant a fry-up or heating canned soup or ravioli—a far cry from my current fridge in London full of fermented delights, among other things. At the time, I was quite proud of my independence, and I was eating food that brought me pleasure.

Every year for my birthday, my mum would make me an enormous, extra-gooey pavlova with raspberries and strawberries. It wasn't at all like the ones you buy in shops or fancy restaurants, where the meringue is really hard and dry: it was soft and delicious, it would melt on your tongue, and it was pure joy. She would also cook a delicious Australian version of lasagna. She'd spent a lot of her youth in the 1950s bravely riding a Vespa in Italy, so she really knew how to make a good one. I loved it, and you would usually find me the morning after, scraping the edges of the pan with the burned cheese crust. I still associate that smell with my happiest memories, and I'd be delighted for my last meal to be just that: a slightly overcooked cheesy lasagna.

What I didn't know then is that these emotional and social associations with our favorite foods are critical. The food we eat as children—even the food we're exposed to in our mother's womb—shapes our food preferences for life. Trying new flavors, foods, and textures is something we have to experiment with as adults, keeping an open mind and a curious palate in the same way you listen to new music or try out the latest TV series. What we eat is so much more than just fuel and is certainly much more than an oversimplification of calories in versus calories out. Understanding that is the first crucial step toward having a better relationship with our food.

Plenty of research now shows that our food environment and social context shape our dietary habits. If we grow up seeing food as an enemy or as a reward, it can be tricky to untangle the feelings of shame, guilt, or reward that are linked to those foods. Many of us don't realize that we desire or avoid certain foods because of the emotional association we have with them. That link can be a result of a fond childhood memory—as with the burned crust of my mum's lasagna—or it can be a result of clever advertising that helps pair a certain food with a desirable feeling or event. I was never taught any of this at medical school, where food was only ever fuel and vitamins.

As I grew older, my food influences began to broaden. At 17, I took a gap year before starting to study medicine and got a job in a mountain hotel restaurant in Tyrol, Austria, armed with a smattering of German from school. My job as the kitchen porter was to do all the washing-up. This was my first experience of the intensity of the kitchen, not to mention the Austrian cuisine, and I loved it. I have memories of mountains of delicious Wiener schnitzel and of rolling enormous strudel prior to baking. These are still my much-loved comfort foods today, and you'll find recipes for them later in the book, albeit now adapted to better suit my health needs.

As I returned to the real world, my relationship with food was deprioritized thanks to the demands of medical school, which took up pretty much all of my time and energy. My diet was terrible. As a junior doctor, most of my meals were in the hospital canteen, which specialized in egg and soggy fries, shepherd's pie, and overcooked spaghetti. As my career progressed, I found myself eating quick meal deals of sandwiches and bags of chips. Breakfast was almost always a bowl of muesli with a bit of skimmed milk: tasteless but necessary fuel for the long shift ahead. It wasn't obvious to me at the time that eating in this way was not great for my health—after all, sandwiches and muesli seemed like sensible choices when compared with fast-food burgers for lunch or doughnuts for breakfast.

I have many happy memories from that time, but while I was a student, my father died of a sudden heart attack in his fifties. His death was totally unexpected: he had also been an academic doctor who had never smoked cigarettes, and although he hated exercise, he was relatively slim. Though this was quite a shock, I never worried too much about my own health or mortality until 30 years later in 2011 when, just a few years younger than my father had been when he died, I had what is known as a mini-stroke (a vascular occlusion in the blood vessels to the eye) while backcountry skiing in Italy. My long recovery left me with high blood pressure that I couldn't ignore, giving me the wake-up call I seriously needed.

During those three months off work, I had double vision and couldn't do much, so I started thinking about how to prevent myself from getting a stroke or heart attack. As I looked into the practical advice that patients get about food from government sites or the internet, it became clear it was either out-of-date, unhelpful, or unrealistic. The more I started digging, the angrier and more upset I became about how misleading this information was. From my medicine and physiology background, I knew the advice didn't stack up—like going on a low-fat diet, counting calories, and exercise being fantastic for weight loss, and many other bits of nonsense. Increasingly, some other things I thought were true came into question: not only were patients being misled, but the shortcomings of my medical training were becoming apparent. We simply hadn't been taught about nutrition. I thought I was a healthy, knowledgeable doctor, but I realized I'd gotten it wrong, and this was quite a shock for me.

Two years earlier, in 2009, I'd first come across the potential role of the gut microbiome at a genetics conference, where an American colleague presented his work on the role of the bacterium *H. pylori* in disease. It would be a leap, but I wondered whether I could study the microbiome as an extension of my own genetics work. We use DNA to identify the microbes that live in our gut, so the same skills in genetics would be useful here. For the next couple of years, I tried to generate interest in the field in the UK, but my grants were rejected, either because the microbiome was wrongly viewed as a passing fad or because I wasn't considered an expert in the field. So I went to the US to get funding, and worked with a great research group at Cornell; this is when the work really took off. I had a hunch the microbiome was important, but it wasn't until 2012, when we got the first early results back from our twins study, that its role really came to light. We found that identical twins had different gut microbiomes, and that this could potentially explain why even these genetically identical clones, who often share their environment closely, develop very different diseases. I realized this could be the key in explaining some epidemiological questions I'd been trying to answer for the previous 20 years.

From there, we discovered two key findings. First, genes only play a small part in which microbes you've got. Second, there are links between metabolic diseases such as obesity and having poor gut health and low gut microbial diversity. Where we had one twin who was slimmer compared with their heavier twin, we identified a couple of microbes that seemed to be protective and only appeared in the slimmer twin. When we put the slimmer twin's microbes into sterile mice and overfed them, we could then stop the mice from gaining excess fat. This was definitely a eureka moment (and I don't have many of these). Other evidence from around the world quickly supported this. There was mounting evidence that the gut microbiome plays a role in many diseases, including heart disease, any form of inflammation, obesity, and food allergies. We managed to finally get funding in the UK to extend this research and found that this phenomenon was true in the UK as well as in the US.

The puzzle pieces started to come together. I now had novel insights from the clinic, which I could bring into my own kitchen to improve my diet and health outcomes. A lot of my early attempts were just trial and error. Initially I went vegan, then I experimented with different foods and learned to cook for myself. More important, I had the gradual realization that by changing my diet, I could improve my mood, my concentration, and my energy levels. As I started to eat better and better, I noticed that my weight was shifting too—though that came gradually, after the more immediate daily benefits.

The food I was eating prior to 2011 was—without my knowing—slowly making me sick. But I came to learn that it was the food I was *not* eating that was the real problem. The lack of fiber and plant diversity and the lack of traditional fermented foods, combined with a higher intake of ready-to-eat, ultra-processed foods in my diet, meant that my body was running on just a few unexciting, generally low-fat, low-flavor, and low-nutrient foods. These were foods that I had previously thought were good for me. Luckily my scientific knowledge and natural skepticism helped me to critically question the myths I had been taught and explore what food really does in our bodies.

My quest to know more was helped considerably when, in 2017, Jonathan Wolf, George Hadjigeorgiou, and I founded the science and nutrition company ZOE, which means "life" in Greek. We set out to understand individual responses to food in the real world by enabling scientific research at an unprecedented scale with remote trials conducted by people in their homes. After a totally unexpected pivot during the pandemic, we used community science and a novel app with the help of my King's College colleagues to understand the symptoms of Covid-19 in millions of people. After those years and many studies, which had a major impact on medical understanding and policy, we refocused on personalized health. By combining our latest science with the results of thousands of our members' at-home tests, ZOE now has a proven program that helps people make smarter food choices for their long-term health.

Thanks to hundreds of thousands of members contributing to this community science, we know much more about how to eat well than we did even 10 years ago. This is science evolving at speed and depth; what's exciting for me is that I've now been able to connect the dots between my scientific work, my personal discoveries in how to eat to feel good, and my long-term mission to share this knowledge widely. Over time, my views have changed with the new science, so just as we adapt to new learnings through our data at ZOE, I approach the principles of Food for Life with flexibility in the knowledge that the research and evidence are sure to evolve further. Our mission at ZOE is one I hold for myself; it was my own health scare on the ski slopes that gave me the wake-up call I needed. Like you, I've had to pluck up the courage to try new things, because all the scientific breakthroughs in the world won't make a difference to you or me unless we step into the kitchen, roll up our sleeves, and put theory into practice.

My early attempts at changing my cooking habits brought small triumphs, big failures, and new rituals. I may be an expert in the clinic, but I was an amateur in the kitchen. In changing my habits, I've discovered the pleasure of eating in accordance with the latest science, and it has helped me resolve constipation, have more energy, improve my mood and concentration, sleep better, enjoy food more, and reduce my belt size after years of meal-deal lunches.

To help me translate the scientific findings and six principles of Food for Life, I've worked with fantastic recipe developers and ZOE nutritionists, including Georgia Tyler and Dr. Federica Amati, to create a set of delicious, achievable recipes that bring the latest science into your life and kitchen every day. This is the book I wish I'd had a decade ago. Using it as a guide, with its tips and inspiration, I could have become smarter in the kitchen and healthier a lot quicker. I hope that's what it does for you.

Back to Basics: The Six Principles of Food for Life

Writing and researching the scientific A–Z of food in *Food for Life* was a mammoth task that took me six years to complete, mainly because the subject is so diverse and complex. As I dived into the mysterious, big wide world of brassicas, nuts, seeds, herbs, mushrooms, fish, and eggs, and more, I soon realized why no one else—to my knowledge—had been daft enough to attempt it. Untangling the latest evidence and scientific understanding of how food impacts us and why is no mean feat.

The deeper I got into my research, the more my curiosity led me down new and unexpected paths. It had already become clear to me that our food choices are the most important way that we can influence our gut and overall health, but writing the book also made me realize the huge impact that our food choices have on the environment. From there, I explored the ways we can improve our health while also helping the planet and making better ethical decisions to help animals and other humans.

By the time I came to publish *Food for Life*, I had landed on six key guiding principles that have helped me—and I hope will help you—eat smarter. I don't see them as rigid rules but as a broad framework that, when taken as a whole, comprises an achievable, practical, and enjoyable new way of eating.

1. Eat 30 Plants a Week: All About Abundance

In the quest for optimal health, the gut microbiome plays a central role as the conductor leading the symphony of our bodily functions. From digestion and metabolism to immune function and even to influencing our dietary choices, our gut microbes ensure that each section of the body's orchestra plays in harmony. As part of the American/British Gut Project team investigating the role of the gut microbiome in health, my colleagues and I asked thousands of generous volunteers to mail us their poop. What I discovered is that the diversity of plant species in our diet is more crucial for gut health than the specific type of diet we follow (vegan, pescatarian, carnivore, etc.). Consuming a variety of about 30 different plant species each week emerges as a key strategy for nurturing a healthy gut microbiome and, by extension, overall well-being. Our microbial maestro is a chemical genius that requires a diverse range of foods to create all the subtle melodies and harmonies of our health.

The science behind 30 plants a week

The gut microbiome is the name for the community of microscopic organisms that live in our intestines, mostly our lower large intestine, or colon. It forms a complex ecosystem, home to trillions of microorganisms including bacteria, viruses, phages, fungi, and parasites that influence everything from digestion to immune function. Bacteria are not the most abundant but are the ones we know most about; for example, they act as mini-pharmacies, creating thousands of useful chemicals from the raw materials of the food that reaches them.

A diverse microbiome made up of many different species that can produce a rich variety of chemicals is a tough, resilient one. As well as a diverse mix, you also want to maximize the number of healthy microbes and reduce the number of unhealthy ones. The science and nutrition company ZOE, which I co-founded in 2017, now has the largest collection of detailed gut microbiome data in the world. At ZOE, we recently analyzed over 35,000 stool samples and identified thousands of bacteria that are *entirely new to science*. Previously we were able to spot links between 15 "good" and 15 "bad" bacteria and specific health outcomes. Now we can link 50 "good" and 50 "bad" bacteria to specific health outcomes. Although many of the newly identified bacteria are so new they don't yet have a name, we can see how they're strongly linked to the health of ZOE members. From this data, we've been able to suggest with better accuracy what foods our members should be eating for their specific bacterial community.

Overall, a diet rich in a variety of plants provides a smorgasbord of nutrients and fibers that selectively feed beneficial microbial species. Each plant species offers a unique combination of hundreds—or sometimes thousands—of chemicals made up of fibers, polyphenols, vitamins, and minerals. These collectively support a diverse microbial community, which in turn manufactures a wide range of healthy chemicals. Nothing goes to waste in the microbial mini-pharmacy.

Why 30, though? The number isn't arbitrary. We have shown that individuals consuming roughly 30 different plant species per week have a more diverse microbiome than those who eat around 10 (which is what the majority of us tend to eat). It didn't matter whether the person also ate dairy, fish, or meat; it was the number of plants on their plate that mattered. This diversity is associated with better health outcomes, including reduced inflammation and a lower risk of common diseases. The variety of plants we eat ensures that we're not just feeding a few microbial species, but rather supporting a much wider array, which maximizes our health beyond the gut. A rich microbiome can help regulate appetite and body weight, potentially reducing the risk of obesity, but it can also enhance the body's ability to fight infections and reduce the risk of autoimmune diseases.

This simple yet profound shift in our approach to eating can have far-reaching health benefits. As we learn to embrace the variety that nature offers, and avoid the trap of eating the same foods, we not only nourish our bodies but also contribute to a more sustainable and vibrant food system. I've been communicating the "30 plants a week" idea for a while now, and I've seen that it's been a hugely successful message; it's such a simple idea that resonates with so many people, and it has helped me improve the variety of plants I eat myself.

Eating more plants to improve our health is not a new science. There are countless studies and large reviews that confirm the positive health effects of eating fruits and vegetables, legumes, whole grains, nuts and seeds, and herbs and spices. But until recently, no one focused on the *variety* rather than the *quantity* of plants. There is now plenty of research that eating a greater plant diversity is far better for us than the much-vaunted but boring "five a day," decreasing the risk of illness and improving outcomes for brain function, nutrient status, gut health, and more.

Because we didn't know much about the gut microbes previously, these plant foods were thought to be beneficial mainly because of their micronutrient content—with particular focus on a few vitamins that led to very successful supplements. Sadly, they are only successful commercially, not healthwise, and if anything, very high doses of these individual vitamins in supplement form can do more harm than good. On the other hand, eating a wide variety of plants that contain these vitamins (and much else besides) provides the right dosages and is a far better approach.

A few decades ago, scientists focused on the powerful effects of a few individual chemicals found in plants, known as phytochemicals (*phyto* means "plant" in Greek). For example, sulforaphane in broccoli or beta-carotene in, unsurprisingly, carrots. While these specific plant chemicals do play an important role, they aren't the sole drivers of the wonderfully complex and persistent impact that plants have on our health. This is because plants like these contain thousands of different chemicals of potential benefit, not just the "stars" we talk about because we measured them first. We're now beginning to understand that it's the complex combinations and interactions of fibers, phytochemicals, and plant proteins that make plants so unique.

I find it fascinating that our digestive system has evolved with our gut microbes over millions of years precisely to give them a comfy home with the space (large surface area of the gut) and time (longer length of the gut compared with other mammals) to break down and use all the different nutrients effectively. We can't do this ourselves because we don't make the enzymes necessary to break down plant fibers and transform phytochemicals. So we *need* our gut microbes, and they have evolved to do some vital jobs for us while in residence. They have 500 times more genes than we do, and they're incredibly versatile at interacting with the food we eat while leaving nothing to waste.

But many microbes are fussy about their favorite foods, and specific strains increase rapidly when we eat that particular food. A great example we discovered recently in our research with ZOE is a super-fussy microbe, *Lawsonibacter*, that only grows if you feed it coffee (regular or decaf). It has potential health benefits that people who drink only tea may not enjoy. But that's not to say tea drinkers don't benefit from other plants in other ways.

Cohort studies from Belgium and the Netherlands, as well as our UK study of twins and the American/British Gut Project, have found that eating more fiber and plants is strongly correlated with good gut microbe health. And so the message of "30 plants a week" was born. It aligns well with growing evidence that the promotion of five fruit and vegetables per day hasn't really been cutting it. While five portions of fruit and vegetables a day can still have a positive impact on health, even if you do manage it, without the mention of variety, you are likely to keep repeating the same dull routine. So it is not likely to deliver anything like the same benefits in areas such as reducing the risk of bowel cancer or improving brain function as the 30-plants-a-week approach.

How to eat 30 plants a week

Embracing a diet with 30 different plant species each week encourages culinary creativity, and it's not as difficult as you might think. It invites us to expand our palate beyond the usual suspects of what we traditionally view as "plants" to include a broader range of vegetables, fruits, grains, nuts, seeds, herbs, and spices. This not only benefits our gut microbes, but also enriches our culinary sensory experience, and the recipes in this book will help you cast a wider net.

But it's not just about quantity: the quality of plant-based foods matters too. Opting for whole, minimally processed plants ensures that we get the full spectrum of nutrients they have to offer. Incorporating fermented foods like sauerkraut or kimchi can introduce beneficial live microbes in food (probiotics), further enhancing gut health (more on that later).

The thousands of edible plants that are available to us offer a huge variety of nutrients and healthy phytochemicals/polyphenols compared with all the animal species we normally eat, so it's not a huge surprise that diets rich in many different plants are clearly linked to better health and increased longevity. The Mediterranean diet and diets characterized in the Blue Zones (areas where the highest concentration of healthy centenarians live) differ in ingredients, but they all follow a predominantly plant-based approach.

Spices and herbs also count toward your 30 plants a week. Although they are traditionally eaten in much smaller quantities than, say, root vegetables or leafy greens, these intensely flavorful, aromatic ingredients have an extra-high concentration of plant chemicals, and even in small amounts provide further benefits when you add them to your food. A study known as "the Singapore trial" was one of the first to show just how powerful a couple of teaspoonfuls of mixed curry spices per day can be for the gut microbiome. The men in the trial had their microbiome sequenced throughout the trial, and the positive changes in their gut microbe population were impressive, impactful, and achieved in only two weeks.

Eating a wider variety of plants is really about increasing what you offer your gut microbes by adding to what you already eat. This is definitely not about eliminating your firm favorites: If you love celery, apples, bananas, carrots, and cucumbers, that's wonderful. Just don't forget they won't provide everything your gut microbiome needs for optimal health. However, a complete and rapid overhaul with lots of unfamiliar plants could be stressful for your gut in the short term, which is why making simple, easy additions is a good starting point. Making the change slowly will give your gut time to adapt to the extra fiber.

One handy tip is to include a mirepoix base in your cooking: chopped celery, garlic, onions, and carrots sweated in extra-virgin olive oil is a great way to routinely introduce more flavor, polyphenols, and fiber to your meals. Studies have shown that combinations like these release even more healthy polyphenol chemicals for your microbes than when used individually. Nuts and seeds are another important high-fiber, high-omega-3 fatty acid, and high-polyphenol addition that has been shown to improve heart disease risk, so think about ways you could up your plant numbers, perhaps by adding a handful of nuts to a salad or some mixed seeds to your breakfast granola and yogurt. And alongside ground spice blends, whole-seed spices like coriander, cumin, fennel, and caraway are all nutritious—and delicious.

My experience of eating 30 plants a week

I have found the 30-plants-a-week principle really empowering. I was never particularly inspired by the five-a-day idea, as I usually achieved it easily with a banana, corn, onion, garlic, and a sugary orange juice each day. It also made me lazy when it came to my weekly food choices. I had no clue that nuts and seeds could be such a healthy addition to dishes, and I thought herbs and spices were window dressing. It was exciting to realize that so many things I hadn't considered before—like dark chocolate, coffee, and fresh herbs—were plants that could contribute to the diversity of my diet. Once I realized this, my search for variety became a hobby, exploring greengrocers, international supermarkets, and spice shops for novel plants to add to my repertoire. Trips abroad also became treasure hunts for new plants to savor.

Using more spices and herbs in my dishes added flavor and increased my love of food. One easy hack I learned was to keep a jar in my kitchen, filled with as many different nuts and seeds as I could find, and to keep topping it up. I dip into this every day, adding it to my breakfast kefir and any salads. At ZOE, inspired by this idea, we have used our science and nutrition expertise to create innovative products, including a whole-food 30-plant mix. These products go beyond what you could simply make in your own kitchen, to supercharging the variety of your diet in a simple scoop.

When starting to cook a meal, I nearly always sauté a base of onion, celery, and carrots and then garlic with my olive oil. This way, I have at least four or five plants before I even start to add the other ingredients. This can then evolve into a spicy dish by my adding chile flakes, ginger, and Asian spices, or something more Mediterranean in style by my adding more herbs and tomatoes. What I love about the recipes in this book is that they make adding plants easy, without even thinking about it. If you're like me, you'll become more confident in adding spare vegetables to dishes to enhance the flavor and create leftovers for tomorrow.

The takeaway

The beauty of changing the message from "daily fruit and vegetable" to "30 plants" is that it encourages us to include a much wider variety of foods. Traditional fruits and vegetables are still very much on the menu, but now they have lots of tasty and interesting friends to join them. Many of us hardly ever eat plants like beans and other legumes, whole grains, or mushrooms. With 30 plants a week in our sights, we can be more imaginative, and I want you to welcome some of these wonderful ingredients back onto your plate. You'll also get a boost from knowing that a teaspoon of exotic spices, a handful of nuts, a cup of coffee or green tea, a square of dark chocolate, and even an occasional glass of red wine or craft beer will keep you and your microbiome happy. Let us forget the restrictive era of exclusion diets and think instead about the myriad opportunities for including these wonderful foods in our lives.

2. Eat the Rainbow: The Spectrum of Health

The adage "eat the rainbow" is not just a catchy phrase. It encapsulates a fundamental principle of nutrition that emphasizes the importance of consuming a wide range of colorful fruits and vegetables. This spectrum of foods is not only visually appealing but also packed with a rich variety of tastes and nutrients essential for maintaining good gut health as well as good health overall.

The science behind eating the rainbow

The science behind why eating colorful plants is good for you is simple: they're rich in a variety of colorful plant chemicals that include flavonoids, anthocyanins, and carotenoids, which I refer to collectively as polyphenols for ease. These are potent plant defense chemicals that play a crucial role in our overall well-being, and there's poetry in the simple fact that polyphenols increase when a plant grows in adverse conditions. These compounds are found in abundance in foods like deep purple eggplants, bright red peppers, vibrant green zucchini, and sunshine-yellow peaches. Each color and hue in the plant kingdom signifies a different set of chemicals, containing nutrients and polyphenols that benefit the body in unique ways. I was excited to learn there are over 50,000 diverse chemicals in edible plants—more than we could have dreamed of a few years ago.

The significance of eating a variety of plants goes way beyond the traditional and outdated views of nutrition, which still focus on calories, sugars, fats, and proteins. Plants offer a complex blend of chemicals, structures, and flavors, each with a specific role in nourishing our bodies through our gut microbes. Polyphenols give color, taste, tannins, and some bitterness to a plant, and many of them provide the energy and chemical diversity our microbes need to work properly. It is this diversity that is key to a healthy diet: a purple carrot will have different polyphenols than an orange carrot; a red pepper will be different from a green one.

Until recently, we didn't know why this "diversity over quantity" was so important for health, but a 2023 study showed that the more diverse our microbes are, the more efficient our digestive system is at using all the nutrients at its disposal.

Just as good microbes will flourish with a high-plant diet rich in polyphenols, bad microbes will feast on unhealthy foods (especially ultra-processed foods) to make inflammatory chemicals. This means that in a healthy, diverse microbe community, any invading infectious microbes will find nothing left over to eat and are more likely to starve before they can infect us. This is why it's so important to focus on eating the rainbow. By adding a rich variety of plant compounds to our diets, we're welcoming in as many of the good guys as possible and crowding out the baddies at the same time.

Anecdotally (I have not been able to find good scientific studies on this front), many people report that organic produce has more vibrant colors and a richer and more natural flavor. This could be due to the generally higher polyphenol content, which helps with taste as well as nutrition. Unfortunately, pesticides, like polyphenols, are typically found in higher concentrations in the skins of produce. In order to gain as much of the polyphenol benefit from plants as possible, we suggest eating the whole food, including the skin, so eating plenty of plants often means ingesting more pesticides and raises the question: organic or nonorganic?

The debate over organic foods is a long-running and complex one. Organic foods are grown without the use of conventional pesticides, synthetic fertilizers, sewage sludge, or ionizing radiation. Animals that are grown to produce organic meat, fish, poultry, eggs, and dairy products are not given antibiotics or growth hormones. Nonorganic foods, on the other hand, are produced with the aid of these substances, the amounts depending on the country of origin.

One of the primary arguments in favor of organic foods is the potential health benefits. Organic produce tends to contain fewer pesticides, which are linked to a variety of health issues, including neurological problems and certain cancers. Literature reviews and meta-analysis have found that organic crops have higher antioxidant concentrations and lower cadmium levels (a toxic metal), as well as significantly lower pesticide residues (around three- to five-fold) compared with nonorganic crops. Studies also show that polyphenol counts are a third higher on average, likely because the organically raised plants don't have chemical support and must work harder to grow and survive in nature, which is what polyphenols are actually for: plant self-defense. These findings suggest that organic foods have certain potential health advantages. For the planet, the decision is less clear, as yields of organic farms are lower, but they do avoid nitrogen fertilizers, which are environmentally negative to produce.

The higher cost of organic foods reflects the more labor-intensive agricultural practices and the often smaller scale and yield of organic farms. If you can afford it, it is an investment in personal health and environmental sustainability. It also promotes good farming practices, as in most cases, organic farmers are taking better care of their land and produce. If you want to reduce your exposure to pesticides but worry about cost, you may want to pay a premium for specific organic plants that would normally have very high chemical levels. If there's one place I'd encourage you to spend extra on organic if you can, it would be oats and rye—as they're grown in damp conditions and therefore extensively sprayed with pesticides—or berries with thin skins such as strawberries; but I wouldn't worry too much about thick-skinned oranges, for example.

Organic rainbows may well be a bit brighter, but my key message is that we should all be eating more colorful plants, and whether the plants are organic should be a secondary goal. Organic foods are generally more expensive, which can be a barrier. Organic canned and frozen plants tend to be more affordable than fresh options and are a wonderful way to add more color to your plate—canned beans in water and mixed frozen berries are staples in my kitchen. Also don't forget that small local farms may follow organic farming practices, but they may not be able to afford the official organic certification. If you have access to farmers or farmers' markets nearby, ask them about their crops and buy locally and seasonally. But if buying organic means you can't add as many plants to your plate, I would always urge you to prioritize diversity and abundance of plants over the organic label.

How to eat the rainbow

Incorporating a variety of colorful plants into your diet is not just about health; it's also about enjoyment and culinary exploration. And *how* you add more color to your plate is a lot simpler than it seems. Replacing bland vegetables like iceberg lettuce with different colorful lettuces and leaves like arugula, red radicchio, and mâche can transform meals both nutritionally and gastronomically. Combining different types of plants, such as squashes with beans, or tomatoes with chickpeas, ensures you're getting a more complete and balanced nutrient profile.

The color of a vegetable can often indicate its nutritional value. Intense dark or bright colors suggest high levels of pigment polyphenols, which are beneficial for health. For instance, purple carrots, sweet potatoes, and regular potatoes contain higher levels of different polyphenols than their lighter-colored counterparts. Dark plants like black olives, blackberries, cocoa, and coffee beans are also high in polyphenols, and root spices such as turmeric and ginger have particularly high levels of polyphenols per gram. Although you don't typically eat them in large amounts, colorful spices like cloves, star anise, and curry powder in your recipes all add different polyphenols to your plate.

Although it's a helpful guide, it's not always as simple as choosing the most colorful option to put on your plate. Many children and adults have an aversion to some fruits or vegetables, which can be due to genetic predispositions, early experiences, and cooking methods. Learning to appreciate the taste of vegetables and preparing them in ways that enhance their flavor can help overcome these barriers, and the recipes in this book will show you how to do this.

My experience of eating the rainbow

As a youngster, I hated beets, probably because of school meals. The majority of color in my diet came from peas or iceberg lettuce, the corn hidden in my tuna sandwich, and my daily banana, as well as some tomato sauce and Branston pickles. As I began to cook for myself, I was wary of cooking more than one type of vegetable (in addition to potatoes), thinking it superfluous if meat was the centerpiece of the dish. It also increased the risk of me messing it up with different cooking times and too many pans. Being told to eat the rainbow before understanding about gut health was too vague a concept for me to take on board.

Nowadays, with meat or fish rarely on the menu, I have plenty of room on my plate. I pick as many colors as I can, opting for a mixed variety of peppers, salad leaves, beans, berries, and more. I do a lot of one-pan cooking, either frying it all together or lightly steaming vegetables. I tend to get my vegetables from smaller shops where I can get small amounts of different colors rather than jumbo bags of the same, and I always look out for something new or different. The simplest and often cheapest way to increase colors is to buy premixed combinations: packs of multicolored peppers are a good example, as are combinations of root vegetables or mixed nuts and seeds.

The takeaway

Eating the rainbow not only supports your gut health and reduces the risk of disease, but it also enriches your diet with a greater range of flavors and textures (and will help you reach your 30-plants-a-week target too). By embracing the full rainbow of plant-based foods, you can enjoy the benefits and considerable pleasures of a nutritious and diverse diet.

3. Pivot Your Protein: Sustainability and Legumes

We are currently a population obsessed with protein. Everywhere you go, there's added protein in the most unlikely foods: added-protein pasta, added-protein yogurts, added-protein cereals, protein bars, and high-protein energy drinks. All of this added protein is aimed at a population 95 percent of whom already surpass the amount of protein they need every single day. By contrast, 95 percent of the population is deficient in fiber. So why the panic about protein? Why are we willing to spend considerably more for "high-protein" versions of common foods? Unlike fat, protein can't be stored for later use, so if it's not used immediately for muscle synthesis, for an immune response, or for repair, it's broken down in the liver and converted to energy that often ends up as excess fat. Ironically, these added-protein foods are more expensive but actually have no added value, at a time when many people are struggling to feed their families. There is also growing evidence to suggest that there is such a thing as too much protein, and overconsuming it can increase your risk of heart disease. We should definitely be focusing our energy and spending power elsewhere.

The science of protein

Proteins are composed of amino acids, which are often referred to as the building blocks of life. There are 20 different amino acids that can form a protein, and 9 of these are considered essential: because our bodies can't make them, we must get them from our diet. They are crucial for supplying our liver and our muscles with the building blocks for protein, as well as making constant repairs to our body. Adequate protein intake supports muscle mass, aids recovery from injury and infection, and contributes to our feeling satiated after meals.

As someone deeply immersed in the world of science and nutrition, I appreciate the critical role that protein plays in our diets. It's more than just a nutrient: it's a fundamental building block of life, essential for the growth, repair, and maintenance of our bodies. My journey through the evolving landscape of food science has revealed the importance of protein, not just in regard to quantity but also to quality and source.

Traditionally, when people think of protein, they think of meat and animal products. There's a lot of talk about complete proteins and having "all" of the amino acids in animal-based foods, yet it's also a fact that all plants (yes, all) contain all 20 amino acids. The only difference is in the relative balance of the amino acids. For that reason, people who eat a diet plentiful in a variety of plant-based foods—as ZOE and I advocate—get all of the amino acids and proteins they need. And they live longer and healthier lives than those who eat more animal-based foods to get their protein. The key word here is *variety*.

Not all vegetarians are healthy. They don't all eat a rich diversity of plants, and this can put them at a disadvantage versus omnivores who, by eating meat, will guarantee a good balance of amino acids.

As an epidemiologist and a clinician, I've seen how protein deficiency impacts sick or elderly people, leading to muscle wasting, weakened immunity, and overall poor health. But in contrast, I have never heard of a healthy vegan who was diagnosed with protein deficiency.

Because eating too much meat is associated with an increased risk of mortality and ill health, it's the *source* and the *quality* of protein that is the key consideration from a health perspective for me. The average American eats 329 pounds of meat per year, which is 1.5 times more than in healthy countries like Italy or Japan at 222 pounds per year. In China, the opposite scenario is seen, where meat and dairy consumption is rising fast, as are lifestyle- and diet-associated diseases.

However, when I now think about the overall value of meat- and dairy-based proteins in relation to plant-based proteins, I'm increasingly conscious of the cost to the planet. We now have vastly more animals on the planet bred for our plates than are roaming wild, and we raise and slaughter around 60 billion chickens a year. In *Food for Life*, I discussed the environmental impact and sustainability issues for various protein sources. For example, a pound of protein produced from beef has up to 100 times the carbon cost of a pound equivalent from peas. It's not surprising that reducing your meat intake is the single most important change you can make to help save our planet, far outweighing other potential choices such as giving up your car or flying on planes.

Most of us now know that greenhouse gas emissions from livestock are a significant contributor to climate change. Methane from cow flatulence, nitrous oxide from manure, and carbon dioxide from deforestation and the energy-intensive processes of farming all add up. On top of that, this land could be used for forests or growing vegetables for human, rather than animal, consumption. Beef and lamb have the highest carbon footprints per pound of protein, with beef being about 73 times worse than soy protein in terms of emissions. Even chicken, which is often touted as a more environmentally friendly meat option (because chickens are squashed together), produces six times the emissions of plant-based proteins.

The environmental problems don't end with the consumption of meat. The costs of dairy farming are also high. Dairy farming is second only to meat production in terms of its contribution to global warming; the fishing industry also has a significant environmental footprint. Overfishing has depleted wild fish stocks, and fish farming often devastates marine ecosystems—it requires feed made from wild-caught fish—which exacerbates the sustainability problem. Only shellfish like mussels and clams appear totally sustainable.

In response to these challenges, there is a growing market for alternative proteins. Plant-based diets, which emphasize the consumption of high-protein foods such as lentils, legumes, beans, whole grains, nuts, seeds, and mushrooms, offer a way to reduce our reliance on animal protein. These foods have a lower environmental impact and provide beneficial phytochemicals. Innovations such as lab-grown meat, fermented plant mixes with a high amino acid content, and insect protein are also emerging as sustainable alternatives to traditional animal products.

The environmental impact of our food choices is undeniable, but as consumers, we all have the power to drive change through our dietary choices. We know that eating meat and dairy in large quantities is not good for our health, and we know that producing meat and dairy is bad for the environment. The reason I'm obsessed with legumes is because they offer a tasty, near-perfect solution. They are a vital component of global food security and sustainable agriculture. These plants (also called pulses), which include beans, peanuts, lentils, and peas, are an affordable source of plant-based protein and essential nutrients, which are instrumental in preventing and managing nutrition-related diseases such as obesity, diabetes, and heart conditions. Moreover, legumes can help reduce the impact of climate change through their ability to fix nitrogen in the soil and release soil-bound phosphorus, enhancing soil fertility often without the need for chemical fertilizers. I am happy to be a legumophile.

Despite legumes' numerous advantages, their consumption has been declining globally because of the preference for ultra-processed foods and staple crops like rice and corn. Legumes are rich in protein, zinc, iron, and folate, plus they're low in fat and high in fiber. Many international agencies, such as the World Health Organization, recommend increasing our legume consumption, ideally on a daily basis, and I agree with them. When combined with grains like barley, wheat, or corn, they provide a comprehensive nutrient profile that's good for us and for the planet.

How to pivot your protein

In my work with ZOE, I've learned that for most of us, lack of fiber is far more of an issue than lack of protein. Any food and drink company that says you need an exact amount of a protein drink 30 minutes after exercise or you'll "suffer" is just bamboozling you. Evolution has produced a much more natural, flexible system to recover and repair our body after exercise that does not require energy drinks or instant protein. It merely requires a balanced amount of protein by the end of the day. It's important to realize that it's hard to avoid protein in your diet.

Personalized nutrition is about understanding and respecting our bodies' unique needs and responses. As we look to the future, the role of protein in our diets will continue to evolve. Advances in technology will enable us to measure and tailor our protein intake more precisely to our individual needs. We'll have a better understanding of how different proteins affect our metabolism and health, allowing us to make informed choices that benefit not only ourselves but also the planet.

In the meantime, the important point for you to remember is that while protein is an integral part of our diet, it's not just about consuming it in the right quantity. It's about choosing the right types of *high-quality* protein that align with your health goals, ethical considerations, and the sustainability of our planet. As I continue to explore the world of nutrition, I want to empower others to make informed food choices, with protein playing a central role in that journey.

My biggest piece of advice is to concentrate on eating a variety of nutrient-dense whole foods that will take care of your protein needs at any age. If you're keen on getting into shape and embarking on a very physical, tough workout regimen to build a large amount of new muscle mass, the strenuous physical activity will make you hungry, resulting in your eating more of the nutrient-dense foods that will provide you with all the protein you need. If you are calorie restricting while trying to bulk up, then you might need extra protein from high-protein foods like edamame, tofu, eggs, and lentils. If in doubt, rather than synthetic protein bars or supplements, add these ingredients to your list: nuts, edamame, natural yogurt, cheese, kefir, beans, lentils, peas, mushrooms, tofu, eggs, and, if you eat them, small amounts of good-quality meat and fish.

My experience with protein

After my mountain incident in 2011, my first thought was to try to eat healthily by going vegan. I thought meat and dairy were the main problem with my diet, so I cut them out. I ate lots of vegetables but also lots of bread and white rice, and although I lost some weight, this diet didn't feel sustainable. I also really missed my

fermented dairy products, especially savory cheese, and so I gave up after six weeks. I made lots of mistakes in those early years because I still had not grasped the key principles I'm discussing here. I didn't understand how you could get all the protein you require from plants by selecting the right combinations and embracing variety.

In the last few years, I've come to understand which foods contain all the protein I need. This means if I decided to go vegan for a while, I would have no problems. I've learned to use interesting ingredients, such as adding nutritional yeast to dishes instead of cheese, using soy creams to soften a dish, or adding tofu or tempeh as meat or cheese substitutes. Some protein advocates believe we need as much as 30g of protein at each meal to optimize protein metabolism and maintain good muscle mass. These scientists are focused on short-term muscle building and repair rather than long-term health issues, and there is still plenty of debate on the trade-offs.

The key is to understand that protein is in virtually every whole food, and you should try to select the best ones when you have a choice. With a good mix of plant protein sources and eating hardly any meat, I tested myself with the ZOE food frequency questionnaire and am now comfortably getting all the protein I need, which works out to nearly 1g of protein per kilogram of body weight over the day. My go-to breakfast of yogurt, kefir, and nuts and seeds gets me to roughly 30g of protein, and a light lunch of lima beans or chickpeas with quinoa also works. One portion of cheese gets you around 15g, and a hard-boiled egg around 6g, while in contrast an average slice of bread only provides around 1g of protein.

If you don't eat dairy or meat or fish, you need to take a bit more care and try to eat more nuts and legumes. Remember that soybeans are a great flexible source of protein, with a single portion of tofu providing 8g.

The takeaway

The next time you're building a delicious meal, remember that all plants contain protein. Getting enough high-quality protein in our diet is easily done if we eat enough whole foods, especially legumes, and eating varied, nourishing meals will also help improve the overall nutrient profile of that meal.

As the global population grows and our climate crisis continues, embracing healthy meat substitutes will be more important than ever. Try to explore new foods with an open mind and to understand the nutritional value of different plant ingredients and how they vary in protein so widely. I struggled initially to improve my diet, as I lacked the key understanding of gut health and the role of protein nutrition. Today, if forced to call my diet choices something that fits a label, I use the term "flexitarian," as I occasionally eat meat and fish. But a key reason I wanted to write this cookbook was to make the transition to predominantly plant-based eating easy and healthy. In doing so, I want to showcase some of the modest, less well-known stars—such as legumes—and make them an exciting, delicious, and—most important—easily integrated part of your week.

4. Think Quality, Not Calories: Food Culture and Ultra-Processed Foods (UPFs)

We live in a world where convenience and speed often trump quality, and nowhere is this more evident than in our diets. Ultra-processed foods, or UPFs, have become a staple of modern consumption, but at what cost? These foods are not processed in the way that things like cheese or canned tomatoes are: they are fundamentally altered from their original state; engineered to appeal to our taste buds with unnaturally high levels of fat, sugar, and salt and stripped of essential nutrients. The clear distinction between processed foods and ultra-processed foods is this: processed foods simply make whole foods more convenient to store or cook with, whereas *ultra*-processed foods are fake foods, created in industrial factories using unrecognizable ingredients, stuck together to look like food. They should really be labeled "edible food-like substances." Take a tangy cheese tortilla chip: it looks and tastes nothing like corn on the cob, and yet it is made with "corn" and dozens of other ingredients to enhance its flavor and shelf life before being shaped into a triangle and covered in fake orange coloring.

The term "ultra-processed" was coined to describe these industrial formulations, which are typically devoid of whole foods and are often ready to consume or heat up. They're designed by food chemists to hit the perfect "bliss point," lighting up our brain's pleasure centers and bypassing our body's signals of fullness. When eaten regularly, this can lead to a lack of nutrients in the diet, overconsumption of energy, weight gain, worse mental health, and a host of health and gut issues. Most (but not all) UPFs are also what are known as hyperpalatable foods, in that they are easy to chew and contain three specific combinations of fat and salt, sugar and fat, and sugar and salt that never occur in nature. These are engineered by food scientists to make us overeat them, with the sole purpose of making more profit. The presence of these foods in our system has steadily increased since the 1980s as food companies formulated them and then aggressively marketed them to us.

The science behind UPFs

Research has now clearly shown that UPFs make us feel hungrier, lead us to eat faster and overeat throughout the day, and are associated with an increased risk of disease, mental illness, and earlier death. This happens through a range of mechanisms, including the hyperpalatable combinations of fats, sugars, salt, and carbs that artificially reward our brains, the soft textures that make these foods easier to eat, the lack of fiber and structure, and the effect of all the chemicals on our gut microbes. The impact on our children is particularly alarming, with studies highlighting the detrimental effects of UPFs on their health and development at critical stages of life.

Despite the mounting evidence, our governments have been desperately slow to act. Recommendations such as those from the 2021 UK National Food Strategy to tax nutrient-lacking, ultra-processed snack foods have been vetoed, leaving us stuck in an escalating food health crisis as real food costs have risen rapidly beyond those of fake foods. Encouragingly, over 10 more enlightened countries now include UPFs in their list of foods to avoid in national guidelines. Globally, change is afoot.

The science on UPFs is new and evolves every week. The more time goes on, the clearer the relationship between consuming these foods and poor health outcomes is. The primary issue with UPFs (and one that is exploited by the food industry) is the lack of consensus on how to spot, define, and compare them. They have very different health profiles, and there are mixed messages between the way that a minority of UPFs (5–10 percent) are currently grouped together in the NOVA classification (the first system to categorize UPFs, invented by Brazilian researcher Carlos Monteiro in 2009). Not all UPFs are created equal: although currently in the same category, baked beans are clearly better for us than an iced sweet bun, as the beans themselves provide plant protein and fiber; and high-fiber cereals or supermarket whole-grain breads are clearly better than a caramel and chocolate dessert.

A minority of UPFs may be less detrimental, but the overwhelming majority of them have no health benefit whatsoever and are actively harmful. Arguing about these anomalies intentionally distracts us from the clear science: eating more UPFs is associated with an increased risk of disease, especially heart disease, mental health disorders, and metabolic diseases. Decreasing their consumption as a whole should be our main focus for improving health. It's almost impossible to avoid them completely, so if we focus on reducing the average intake first, we can then focus on which are better than others. Many South American countries, including Chile and Brazil, have successfully implemented a clear health warning sign for UPFs to help consumers. This way, shoppers can easily identify the foods they should not be adding to their carts.

How to rethink your relationship with UPFs

As individuals, we need to act. In an ideal world we'd expect legislative change at an industry level, but UPF producers lobby hard against it, and we don't have the luxury of waiting for the radical change that's badly needed. So we must educate ourselves on the true nature of the foods we consume while at the same time putting pressure on our politicians to make a change. One practical way to identify an ultra-processed product is to check its list of ingredients for substances and additives rarely used in home cooking. If you see a long list of ingredients you don't recognize, chances are it's ultra-processed. Another clue is that fake food is usually brightly packaged and full of dodgy health claims, such as "high in protein," "1 of your 5-a-day," "low calorie," "low fat," or "added vitamin C." These are called "health halos" and are used to con the public into buying unhealthy food.

The food industry is aware of these issues and the increasing claims that it's acting the same way the cigarette industry did 40 years ago; each year a higher proportion of their profits comes from the most unhealthy foods. They say they're researching ways to make UPFs healthier. But why would they want to voluntarily make their food less addictive and less profitable?

Classifying UPFs is still not perfect in a rigid black-and-white system. Clearly those with 20 added chemicals are much worse than those with just 1 added emulsifier. It's almost impossible to exclude all UPFs from our diets. I would find it awkward and unnecessary depending on the social situation, for example, to always refuse a cookie or a cheese cracker. But we do need to gradually change our habits and our food culture; thankfully, identifying UPFs and thinking about their impact on our diet doesn't have to be daunting. There are many simple guidelines to help you.

When buying food, first ask yourself whether you could make it simply and cheaply at home without the need for industrial ingredients and processes. Commercial salad dressing and mayonnaise, ready-made sauces, stock cubes, and sliced bread are among the biggest UPF culprits, so making your own at home could end up being much healthier and more affordable. Snacks are typically a major culprit when it comes to UPF consumption (even those marketed as "healthy"), so we've included a fantastic Snacks chapter bursting with recipes that you can make at home and bring with you wherever you go. When you do buy something from a shop, like a yogurt, look at the label and think: Should I buy the flavored fruit one with 10 ingredients or the one with just two or three ingredients? The answer becomes much simpler. In this cookbook, we've done our best to steer clear of UPF ingredients in the recipes, instead giving you simple and new ways of cooking without them. For example, you can add depth of flavor to recipes by using the homemade Boosting Bouillon (page 264), miso, or nutritional yeast instead of traditional stock cubes. We're giving you the best chance of creating meals without UPFs, but if you do find yourself adding a stock cube or another UPF, please don't stress about it. They're all around us and have become part of our food environment—even I find it difficult to completely avoid them.

My experience with UPFs

Back in 2011, when the NOVA system was nonexistent, I only had a vague idea of what UPFs were. Around a fifth of our UPF intake comes from mass-produced bread, and I was a loyal customer—as long as it looked brown or had a few health halos on the wrapping. I also frequently ate breakfast cereals that were UPFs in disguise.

As the evidence on UPFs evolved and the interaction of these industrial ingredients with our gut microbiome became clearer, I realized the harm these products could be doing to me and my gut, which led me to look carefully at the labels. Once I did that, I cut back almost immediately. I avoided most supermarket bread and either bought or made my own rye bread, gave up cereals and bagels as a regular breakfast option, and avoided virtually all sweetened drinks. Even for snacks such as potato or vegetable chips, I now scrutinize the label on the package and will pick the least processed one—if it still tastes good (if in doubt, I just pick whole nuts instead). The average adult in the UK and US eats around 60 percent of their food as ultra-processed, and I estimate I've gradually cut this down without any big effort to around 10 percent, which allows me to still have the occasional industrial cookie or cake.

Cutting down on UPFs may sound like a challenge, but for me it wasn't as hard as I thought. Making one decision at a time and then reinforcing that habit, particularly when shopping, meant I was able to cut back gradually. Knowing the damage these UPFs were doing to my body proved excellent motivation, and I soon found that their whole-food replacements were tastier and more enjoyable than I had imagined.

The takeaway

Don't let clever marketing or food scientists trick you into eating fake food that's superficially appealing and impossibly tasty—but little else. Remember, most fake food is designed to be hyperpalatable with precise mixes of salt, sugars, and fats and an easy-to-chew texture that makes us regularly overeat them. I've found that the more I know about the damage they can do to my body, the more easily

I've been able to cut them out. The quality of our food is a beacon that guides us toward optimal health and environmental stewardship. Finding the real quality and rejecting edible food-like substances is about the power of informed choice and the potential for each of us to shape our future through the foods we select.

5. Incorporate Fermented Foods: The Benefits of Microbial Alchemy

If you were to open my fridge in London these days, you'd see that it is packed with an abundance of weird and wonderful ferments on the go. From my go-to kefir and kombucha to other experiments like a fermented mushroom and garlic spread or a homemade labneh, my fridge is further evidence of my passion and zest for ferments. Despite being a feature of our diets for millennia, fermented foods have recently reemerged as a cornerstone for gut health and overall well-being. Fermentation, a process as old as civilization itself, involves the transformation of food by live microbes. This "cold-cooking" method not only preserves food but also enhances its nutritional profile and introduces a symphony of extra flavors.

The science behind fermented foods

The health benefits of fermented foods are rooted in their contribution to supporting gut microbiome health and diversity. Fermented foods like yogurt, kefir, kombucha, sauerkraut, and kimchi are teeming with beneficial bacteria that add goodness to the existing bacteria in your gut when you eat them regularly. Although their presence is fleeting, these microbes act as boosters, stimulating the production of health-promoting chemicals and aiding in metabolism. Yogurt, a well-studied fermented food, is often the poster child for probiotic strains—the live beneficial bacteria that confer health advantages. But not all fermented foods are created equal. Many modern commercial yogurts, especially those marketed for children, are laden with added sugars, artificial sweeteners, and other chemical additives that negate their potential benefits. Traditional fermented foods, on the other hand, are naturally rich in probiotic strains that support gut microbial diversity without the unnecessary additives.

Consuming fermented foods is linked to a plethora of health benefits. For instance, kefir, a fermented milk drink, boasts a microbial composition several times that of yogurt, with up to seven times more strains, offering a more potent probiotic punch. Its health benefits are well documented, ranging from improved digestion to potential weight loss. Similarly, kimchi, a Korean dish of spicy fermented vegetables and multiple microbes, has been linked in many studies with a wide variety of health improvements, including helping maintain a healthy body weight and generally improving the immune system and metabolism.

The evidence supporting the health benefits of fermented foods is not merely limited to anecdotal or traditional claims. Scientific research—including our own from TwinsUK and ZOE studies involving some large community science projects—confirms benefits for energy, mood, and gut symptoms in thousands of people. Moreover, fermented foods do more than support our microbes. The fermentation process itself can break down food components, making nutrients more accessible and aiding digestion. For example, fermentation breaks down the lactose in milk into smaller pieces, making products like cheese, yogurt, and kefir more digestible for those with some form of lactose intolerance (currently around 80 percent of adults on the planet).

How to incorporate fermented foods

Despite the recent and welcome surge in interest in fermented foods, we should view the rapid commercialization somewhat skeptically. The health benefits of fermented foods are often compromised by modern food-processing techniques. For instance, many commercial sauerkrauts are pickled in vinegar, which kills the live microbes, stripping away the probiotic benefits. Similarly, some kombuchas are pasteurized, which kills the live bacteria, or packed with chemicals to give them a long shelf life. Homemade or small-production artisanal fermented foods, where the live microbial content is preserved with minimal additives, are often superior choices, which is why we've included several recipes in the pages that follow to help you get started.

A factor when considering fermented foods is the environmental impact of food production. While dairy-based fermented products like yogurt and kefir offer health benefits and are delicious, they also come with substantial environmental costs due to the milk from dairy herds required for their production. I try to eat dairy as fermented milk, traditional cheese, and natural yogurt from the highest-welfare sources I can find. In the future of food, we should all be looking at nondairy alternatives that can provide similar benefits with a smaller ecological footprint and trying to have dairy foods from the most sustainable possible sources. We've had 10,000 years to perfect fermented foods from dairy but only a few decades for nondairy, and the picture is improving each year. As soon as there is a healthy and tasty nondairy equivalent I love, I will be switching.

On the other hand, plant-based fermented foods are a great tool for reducing food waste because you can ferment just about any plant. Have some leftover cabbage from a dinner recipe? You can ferment that. Leftover rhubarb from a pudding? Ferment it. Spare apple peels? You get the idea. There are endless opportunities—just by adding salt water (or sometimes honey). In the world of fermenting, nothing goes to waste, saving the planet and your wallet.

Whether it's natural yogurt, kefir, or sauerkraut, the best way to incorporate a fermented food if you haven't tried it before is to just add a tablespoon to a meal and build from there. A tablespoon of kimchi stirred into a stew at the end will add crunch and flavor, a tablespoon of kefir stirred into a soup after cooking will add creaminess and tang, a tablespoon of sauerkraut on top of your salad adds complexity and flavor. Small additions every day add up and before you know it, you'll be eating three to five servings without even realizing it. Find the fermented food that works best for you and your body; some find kefir agrees with them best, others swear by red cabbage kraut.

A great place to start if you'd like to experiment with making your own fermented food is sauerkraut. Do give it a try, as it's fun, cheap, and easy and is a great way of using up your veggies at home. Simply shred cabbage, weigh it, and add 2 percent salt (2g of salt for every 3½ oz / 100g cabbage). You then pack it in a jar and leave it for 10 days. My first attempt got me hooked, and I started boldly experimenting with adding herbs and seeds; now I love adding it to salads or soups or eating it with my cheese. Kimchi takes time for most people to get used to, so try to find or make a mild one to begin with that isn't too spicy. As you get used to the amazing flavors, you'll find you can mix it with yogurts, mashed vegetables, cream, or cream cheese with great success. This book brings together many novel ideas for making ferments part of every meal when, in the past, we might have just used cream or less exciting ingredients.

My advice to the fermenting newcomer is to find some commercial fermented products you enjoy and slowly work up to fermenting your own. One fun and low-risk trick is to add the last heaped tablespoon of store-bought kefir to an open container of full-fat milk and leave it at room temperature. If the kefir is good quality, it should solidify the milk and transform it into kefir, which you then keep in the fridge. Our ancestors called this "back-slopping," and it is how many yogurts and cheeses were made, keeping the colonies of microbes alive across generations.

If you don't tolerate fermented foods well, don't worry too much. The other principles of eating in this book will still support your health and gut microbiome happiness very well. But do remember that eating small portions regularly (i.e., little and often), is the healthiest way to enjoy fermented foods, so if you're just

starting out, build up your intake gradually. This will not only allow you to get accustomed to the taste and habit but will also give your body time to adjust to your new probiotic friends.

My experience with fermented foods

In 2011, I was pretty ignorant when it came to this area. I had hardly heard the term "fermented foods" and thought healthy dessert options were the heavily marketed, low-fat, synthetic-tasting soy yogurts with added fake fruit. I had no idea that kimchi was more than a spicy, smelly dish, had not heard of kombucha or kefir, and I had no clue what miso was.

Over the last decade, I have changed slowly to a fermented mindset, and I think many people are starting to do the same. My first change was to swap my artificial low-fat yogurts for full-fat natural ones, and I started having them for breakfast. Then I discovered that kefir was actually a super-yogurt and I shouldn't be frightened of it. It has around seven times the number of microbe species and so has more complex flavors. I initially found it quite sour, so I mixed it with my yogurt for a few weeks; before long I was enjoying the tangy flavors and taking it as a neat shot, although some goat milk kefirs I still find very strong, so I generally stick to cow's milk. Kombucha was my next discovery, and early on I started making my own. I unfortunately left them too long, so they were very sour and acidic and not popular with my friends or family. Undeterred, I kept trying. Gradually I improved and I now have a small shot with my evening meal. There are now plenty of good ones to buy, although the best are not cheap.

Sauerkraut was my next ferment, which I had eaten plenty of during my time in Austria—although back in the 1970s, it was probably pickled rather than fermented, and we never made it ourselves in the restaurant. Trying novel ferments is a treat for my taste buds and gives me an insight into how we might use fermentation to not only create delicious foods but also address the issue of food waste and the impact of food on climate too. I also love that my fridge is always filled with delicious ferments that can turn a simple can of beans or scrambled eggs on toast into an amazing meal full of complex flavors.

The takeaway

We've been eating and storing fermented foods for millennia, and finally the health benefits of preserving and transforming our food this way have been validated by science. We're still learning, but it's clear that by incorporating a rich variety of fermented foods regularly into our diets, we are not just supporting our gut microbiome but are also embracing a human tradition that has nourished our ancestors and helped their immune systems survive countless threats.

6. Try Time-Restricted Eating: Give Your Gut a Break

Sometimes how and when you eat can matter as much as *what* you eat. As a junior doctor on duty for days at a time, like most of my colleagues, I learned how to eat fast—you never knew when you would be called to the next emergency. We now know that the speed of your eating has an effect on how the food is absorbed and how your body responds to it. ZOE research shows that faster eaters consume on average 120 calories more per day than slower eaters and have a higher body weight and increased heart and metabolic disease risk. Other trials have shown that fast eaters are more likely to carry excess abdominal weight, which is linked to having more visceral fat—the type of fat that sits inside your abdominal walls, surrounding your organs, and is linked to poor health.

The habit of overnight fasting, or time-restricted eating (TRE), has grabbed our attention for its potential health benefits, particularly for the gut microbiome. TRE is a dietary approach that aligns with the daily patterns, also known as circadian rhythms, of both our bodies and microbes. It involves eating all of our food for the day within roughly the same time frame during daylight hours and fasting for the remaining hours, typically overnight. I often suggest a fasting period of 12–14 hours as the "sweet spot" for improved metabolism and healthy weight maintenance. Not only does this provide health benefits, it is also fairly sustainable in the long term. For example, you might finish dinner by 9 p.m. and delay breakfast until 11 a.m. the next day, or finish dinner at 6 p.m. and have breakfast at 8 a.m.

The science behind TRE

When we fast overnight, we give some of our gut microbes a vacation, allowing them time to rest and rejuvenate. We also give our hardworking gut lining time to repair and produce enough new mucus to protect the delicate gut barrier layer. This microbe rest period is similar to human sleep, where the body has vital time to recuperate and repair itself. This break can also help reduce the overgrowth of certain microbes that thrive on a constant supply of nutrients, promoting a more balanced microbial community. Once the microbes have no more food to eat, the varied day team gets replaced by the night cleaning team, who are a different set of microbes. The night team specializes in eating the sugary layer of the mucus coating of our gut lining. This is like mowing the lawn to keep it growing evenly and healthy, which is critical for the gut barrier to function at its best. This one-cell-thick checkpoint keeps bacteria and other waste products in our gut from leaking into our bloodstream and closely surrounding immune tissues, thereby reducing the risk of inflammation.

Regular overnight fasting is also associated with improved metabolism, such as glucose control and reduced blood fat levels. According to some studies, it can also help with modest weight loss and better healthy weight maintenance. Like humans, our gut microbes have their own circadian rhythms, and by giving them a rest during the night, we're respecting their natural cycles.

The first studies on intermittent fasting were originally in mice, but there are now over 20 clinical studies in humans. While previous studies have shown that there are benefits to TRE, most of the research has only recruited small groups of people, usually men—many of whom have chronic conditions—rather than the general population. To further investigate, in October 2022, my colleagues and I at ZOE launched the largest-ever community experiment into TRE—also known as intermittent fasting (IF)—called The Big IF Study. More than 140,000 people signed up to see if TRE might work for them and how it impacted their bodies. During the course of the study, the participants didn't change *what* they ate, only *when* they ate.

For the first week, participants ate as they normally would, and for the final two weeks, we asked them to eat during a 10-hour window, thus fasting for 14 hours. Outside their eating windows, they only consumed water, black tea, or black coffee.

When we analyzed the results, it was clear that TRE had made a positive impact. On average, participants reported an 11 percent increase in mood and a 22 percent increase in energy, compared with their baseline before starting TRE. I was surprised that 64 percent of participants reported that their symptoms of bloating improved, and 58 percent consumed fewer snacks during the TRE intervention. There was also a slight drop in reported hunger. But delaying your breakfast or having an early supper doesn't suit everyone. From our study, it looks like a third of people find it easy, and a third find it really tough. Several of my ZOE colleagues found it made them grumpy and hungry, and some people reported it made them a bit too obsessed about mealtimes. You don't have to fast to be healthy, so don't get upset if it's tricky or you are worried about it becoming an obsession. Time-restricted eating is not advised for pregnant women, those who are undernourished, and people who are living with type 1 diabetes. So, listen to your body and any guidance that might apply to your circumstances, and then, if it feels like something you'd like to try, give it a go. And never skip a dinner with friends because it's outside your eating window!

How to incorporate TRE into your lifestyle

Our response to fasting, like our response to food, is highly personal, so my advice for how to incorporate it into your life is quite simple: give it a try for a few days for 12–14 hours overnight, pay attention to your body's reaction, and explore if it suits you or not. You may need a few weeks to adjust. If you find it easy, it's a great way to eat healthier without much effort. Stay curious and note how it makes you feel. Once you find what works for you, follow that pattern regularly and you are likely to see some benefit.

I'm often asked what people can drink during a fasting period. There is surprisingly little research around this. The main principle is that you shouldn't eat or drink anything that requires digestion and triggers a metabolic response that requires our body to work and break down foods and absorb nutrients. The consensus among fasting scientists is that black tea or black coffee are fine, as are green tea and water, as long as they contain no milk, sugar, or chemical sweeteners. Some experts believe that avoiding sweetness is key, and if herbal tea is naturally sweet or contains bergamot like Earl Grey, it should be avoided. Some people complain that they like a drop of milk in their tea or coffee and it surely won't do any harm. The truth is, we don't yet have all the answers and it may be different for each person. If that single drop of milk helps you to fast sustainably, then I would continue, at least until the science catches up.

My experience with TRE

My first experiences of fasting were about 10 years ago when the 5:2 diet plan was at its height. Like many others, I tried it out and found that two days a week of calorie restriction—knowing that you could eat what you liked the next day—was easier than I thought. This was important psychologically. But it was not true fasting, because on the two days, although you were only allowed to eat 500 calories, there were no time restrictions. Studies subsequently showed this was a popular way of losing weight but was less useful in the long term. For most people, it was really hard to stick to, and they had similar results to diets that restricted calories daily—the hunger signals eventually won and the plan was abandoned. TRE was something I first tried around 2017, and I initially kept it simple. For two weeks, I just skipped breakfast and had a slightly earlier and more substantial lunch. I found that I wasn't hungry when I woke up, and this seemed to suit me, as long as I was allowed black coffee or black tea. I still sometimes skip breakfast, and studies have shown that contrary to myth and official guidelines, it is perfectly safe to do so.

Back in 2017, there were only a few studies on mice, showing that by compressing their eating window, they could improve health parameters and stop weight gain. I didn't totally believe them alone, as mice eat and behave very differently from humans. Even so, I was intrigued enough to want to try it. I liked the idea that you weren't restricting calories and could eat what you liked within your eating window. Although the data shows that theoretically finishing your evening meal early and then having an early breakfast work best (i.e., an early fast), my routine and social life meant that a late fast of 14 hours suited me much better. I found that just by thinking about meal timings, you're more likely to forgo that late-night piece of cake or cookie. I now try to have a small piece of dark chocolate at the end of my meal rather than an hour or two after. In general, combining snacks with meals appears to be better for your body.

There are a few people who can fast for 18 hours and feel very good with impressive results, but they are definitely a minority. I now routinely try to have breakfast after 11am and finish my evening meal by 9 p.m. This gives me more energy and makes me feel sharper in the mornings. Sometimes if I have a podcast recording at midday, I'll delay eating until after 2 p.m. But to be sustainable for years, such a system has to be flexible. If my dinner runs late, I'll push back my breakfast or combine it with lunch and have a brunch instead. I find that if I skip a morning meal at home completely, it's difficult for me to get all the fermented foods and plant variety I need, so for me it is still a tasty and useful meal. Sometimes there are social and culinary opportunities that are just too good to miss, even if they're not at the perfect time for you. I've often succumbed to a fantastic breakfast buffet in a hotel a bit earlier than I would have liked, but life is also about enjoyment and spontaneity, so it's important to stay flexible.

The takeaway

Overnight fasting is a great way of supporting the health of your gut microbiome and helping your mood and energy levels. It may also improve other common symptoms of poor gut health, such as bloating or constipation. By aligning with our natural circadian rhythms, TRE can help maintain a balanced microbial community, support our metabolism, and allow us to maintain a healthy weight. As research continues to evolve, personalized approaches to TRE will become more refined, allowing you to tailor your eating patterns to your specific needs, biorhythms, and gut microbiome profiles.

How to Use This Book

Keeping that perfect blend of science and pleasure as a priority, I've worked with my team at ZOE to create a cookbook of recipes that live and breathe the six core Food for Life principles, while balancing ease of use and cooking practicalities with enjoyment and taste. Together, these 100+ recipes demonstrate the enormous scope and possibilities—as well as the simplicity—of eating the Food for Life way.

I've included some of my favorites from my past, like a twist on my mother's lasagna recipe (see Juno's Lasagna on page 203). Mine is packed with lentils and mushrooms to replace the meat, and it's perfect for a big party or family gathering. I'm delighted to report that my French-Belgian wife, who is usually a tough critic of meat-replacement dishes, loved this one, asked for seconds, and even took some to work the next day. What a relief! I've also added updated versions of my favorite Wiener schnitzel and apple strudel from my time as a teenager working in the kitchen in Austria (see pages 164 and 237).

When thinking about how to organize the chapters, I was influenced by my own experience of changing the way I eat, and also the common requests that we hear from ZOE members. In order for us to change the way we eat permanently, we need recipes that genuinely reflect our needs and tastes, so as well as recipes for mornings, satisfying mains, vibrant salads, and sweet treats, you'll find meals that can be rustled up in under 15 minutes, ideas for entertaining when you have friends and family around, meals that can be put together after a raid of your pantry, and even snacks to enjoy when hunger calls.

Every recipe has had to work hard to earn its place here. Together, they exemplify the Food for Life principles, the way I now eat, and the key advice we give to ZOE members:

- Eat 30 plants a week
- Eat the rainbow
- Pivot your protein
- Think quality, not calories: minimize UPFs
- Incorporate fermented foods
- Try time-restricted eating

Each recipe is packed with fiber and plant diversity and includes a plant count, giving a real feast for your gut microbiome. This plant-first approach will help you

get to your 30 different plants a week, and we always encourage plant swaps for adaptability. The plant count is designed to help you increase the diversity of fibers and polyphenols in your diet based on our current ideas of how to contribute to your 30-plants-a-week target. Each plant food that contains fiber and polyphenols is included, and we also include an approximate amount of fiber per recipe in 5g incremental measures, to help you increase your intake. Be aware that this figure is approximate and will depend on various factors, such as the brand of beans or even the particular carrot you use. Remember, average intakes are currently less than 20g per day for the UK and US—we should be aiming for 30–50g per day. Our gut microbes love prebiotic plant fiber, and the recipes in this book will go a long way toward providing them with what they need.

We've also tested each recipe, not only for its flavor and ease of use, but also for its ZOE Score. These are calculated for each member using their results from at-home tests and questionnaires. The tests analyze blood fat, blood sugar, and gut microbiome health, as well as diet quality and personal data, to score food from 0 to 100 to help members make smarter food choices. Higher scores are more favorable, which can be achieved by adding more diversity and variety to your plate; it's what inspired the name of our Score Boosters chapter. We've designed the recipes in this book to score highly, even for a profile of someone with low blood sugar and fat scores, like me. This means whether you are a ZOE member or not, you can enjoy these meals regularly without worrying about unfavorable blood sugar or blood fat responses, and you can be sure they'll benefit your gut microbiome. For ZOE members, you can look up the recipes to find out how they score for you personally—and with extra detail so you can tweak them further if you wish.

Everyone should be able to cook this wonderful combination and variety of healthy and tasty recipes, even if you're starting with limited skills in the kitchen, like I did. In general, I've found that success lies in preparation and having some favorites that you can cook without any stress. The beauty of these recipes is that many of the ingredients needed to make them can be bought in advance and stocked in your pantry or freezer. We use a lot of canned beans, cooked grains, nuts, seeds, miso, and tahini, which store well. Many of the recipes will only require a few fresh or frozen vegetables and herbs for you to complete them, as we've deliberately tried to make cooking the Food for Life way easy. Mindful of environmental impact and affordability, we've also balanced the recipes with a variety of ingredients so you can either work with the fruits and vegetables that are in season where you live or use canned and frozen alternatives.

You'll notice that meat and fish are suggested as optional extras. If that's what you or your dinner companions prefer, try to think of them as side dishes to the main event, the plant foods. This means the plants are always the centerpiece of the dish, rather than the reverse, which was the annoying scenario I encountered a decade ago when I started reducing my meat intake. Increasingly, more people (including me) are calling themselves "plant-based eaters" rather than strictly vegan or vegetarian. What this means is that the vast majority of the food we eat is whole-food plants but that, occasionally, we may want to try some fish or meat for variety—or, like me, to obtain some extra nutrients like vitamin B$_{12}$, which I need more of. Health- and environment-wise, having occasional cuts of meat isn't harmful if you're otherwise eating enough healthy whole plants. A key message here is about us all eating less meat and fish to both save the planet and keep us healthy. But ethics and animal welfare are a whole other matter, and we have offered vegan, dairy-free swaps throughout the recipes in this book to help you veganize dishes if you choose.

You won't need any major investment in a high-tech kitchen to cook these recipes; the only main kitchen equipment you'll need other than an oven and a stovetop is a food processor and a blender of some kind. If you're a recent convert to an air fryer, you will already know that some vegetables cook well and rapidly in them, saving time and money. When I found myself making an eggplant curry in a rush recently, I was amazed to find the eggplant roasted perfectly in an air fryer in 15 minutes, just sliced in two with a little salt and olive oil. We'll signpost any other time-saving examples or tips within each recipe.

Last, I hope you'll have absorbed by now that my approach to eating is one of abundance, and it's woven throughout these recipes. With that in mind, I encourage you to add in foods rather than exclude them, which I've found to be a fun, liberating, and positive shift in my mindset. For example, rather than forcing yourself to cut out all chocolate or sugar, think about ways that you can still eat them—for example, by adding lots of fiber and nuts. This way, you can enjoy the things you love while helping your body moderate its overall food response, leaving you feeling good for the rest of the day.

Stocking Your Kitchen to Support Success

Before we begin, I wanted to give you a list of ingredients that are useful to always have on hand—in your pantry, fridge, and freezer. I find that having these around makes it much easier to find motivation and get started. Many of these are the underappreciated staples that really come into their own in the 15-Minute Meals and Pantry Raid chapters. Though they're great as emergency last-minute resorts, I like to think of them as the constant companions that I rely on to take the stress out of shopping and healthy cooking. Never underestimate the affordability and nutritional benefits of frozen, canned, and jarred foods. They truly are the unsung heroes of eating well for long-term health, and I always have plenty on standby.

In the pantry

A well-stocked pantry means you invariably have a quick and easy meal at hand. Having an abundance and variety of grains means you've got excellent alternatives to starchy rice and pastas. Cans of beans and other legumes are versatile and affordable, or, for a treat, try jarred beans with their extra-silky texture. Miso and nutritional yeast are great swaps for UPF stock cubes, but you'll also see our Boosting Bouillon listed here as it's found in so many of the recipes. It's easy to make, so stock up and use liberally. Extra-virgin olive oil is the only cooking oil you'll need, and a great tip is to make sure it's stored in as dark a bottle as possible away from sunlight.

- Dried whole grains and legumes: buckwheat, spelt, pearl barley, and mixed quinoa; red lentils
- Flours: spelt flour, whole-wheat flour, chickpea flour
- Oat bran and rolled or steel-cut oats, preferably organic
- Whole-wheat pasta and red lentil pasta
- Eggs (the best quality available to you)
- Canned beans and other legumes, in as many varieties as possible
- Canned vegetables, especially tomatoes and corn
- Jarred vegetables: our recipes include olives, capers, and artichokes
- Nutritional yeast
- Boosting Bouillon (page 264): used in many recipes throughout the book to add depth of flavor
- Extra-virgin olive oil
- Jars of mixed seeds
- Nuts: mixed, unsalted
- Dried fruits: mixed, unsweetened
- Spices and herbs: e.g., cumin, coriander, rosemary, turmeric, paprika, chile flakes, curry powder, bay leaves, Mediterranean herb mix, ginger, sumac
- Vinegar: apple cider vinegar (ACV) or red wine vinegar
- Coffee
- Green tea

In the fridge

My fridge is now full of live cultures and experiments. Making sure you have the four Ks on hand—kefir, kombucha, kimchi, and kraut—is an easy way to increase your fermented food intake. Miso and gochujang—a Korean paste made of red chiles, fermented soybeans, rice, and salt—are both fermented and fantastic at adding depth and flavor.

- Kefir
- Kombucha
- Kimchi
- Sauerkraut
- Fermented vegetables and pickles
- Full-fat natural yogurt
- Miso: any variety will work in these recipes, so choose one you like
- Gochujang or chile paste
- Tahini
- Vegetables, fruits, leafy greens, cabbage
- A little artisanal cheese
- Lemons or limes

In the freezer

Make the freezer your best friend. With a bag of frozen spinach, you've got a great start for a gut-friendly meal. This frozen tundra is actually fertile ground for abundance and diversity, saving you time and money, and managing food waste. I always try to make sure I have a nice thick, Italian-style vegetable soup (see the Minestrone on page 188) in the freezer that I can simply defrost and reheat when I'm pressed for time.

- Herbs: freeze fresh herbs, simply washed or in olive oil, ready to use
- Vegetables: spinach, peas, mushrooms, mixed vegetables
- Mixed berries and fruits
- Mirepoix (make your own or buy it ready-made)

Frequently Asked Questions

People regularly ask me certain questions about the ins and outs of making healthy choices—I'm often asked about what I eat on a normal day, for example. This is one of the trickiest questions I get because my reply now is that I don't have normal days anymore—if you're striving for variety and diversity, you don't want to get tied down to boring routines, like the rut I was in 10 years ago with my identical lunch and snacks every day. That said, I do now have a go-to breakfast that I sometimes eat around midday if I ate late the night before. Because my breakfast video on YouTube has been viewed millions of times now, I've made sure to include it in the Mornings chapter, with plenty of possible swaps and additions. (Note that we haven't called this chapter "Breakfast" in case, like I often am, you're giving your gut a rest.)

Before you get started, I'll share some of my other very common FAQs with you. I hope you can find your answers here; if not, many others are covered in detail in *Food for Life*.

What oil should I cook with?

There's only one oil you need to know about: extra-virgin olive oil, or EVOO. The rest are for those occasions when you might want a specific taste. So, if you're making a Sri Lankan curry, by all means use coconut oil. If you want to do some special high-temperature wok frying, you might use a high-quality canola oil or a peanut oil. If you want a one-off rich dish, you might even want to mix some butter into your olive oil. But 95 percent of the time, you just need one oil—EVOO.

What is one portion of my 30 plants a week?

Surprisingly, we don't yet know for sure. This is something the ZOE team and I are working on with the data our members are sharing with us. But for the moment, generally, our recommended approximate portion sizes look like this: a cup of chopped vegetables, a handful of fresh herbs, a teaspoon of spices, or a handful of nuts and seeds. I suggest you start with these sizes, because if it turns out that a sprig of mint leaves does the trick, so much the better.

Why the obsession with beans and legumes?

Because over the last 30 years, we've been eating less and less of them, and yet they are among the most nutritious plants we can eat in terms of fiber, protein, and nutrients. Even though you can add them to nearly every meal, people in the UK and US are not eating anywhere near as much as they should be. Eating them regularly goes a long way in helping reduce climate change—because they're nitrogen-fixing and they don't need as much fertilizer, and reducing our use of fertilizers that cost a lot of energy to produce is one of the main things we can do to reduce greenhouse gases.

What is the value of canned and frozen versus fresh food?

Canned foods and frozen fruits and vegetables feature heavily in the recipes. They're often cheaper, often fresher, and often have more nutrients than fresh produce—not to mention a much longer shelf life. The only thing to watch out for is whether they have other additives that are unhealthy. Some baked beans, for example, reduce the nutritional value by adding ultra-processed sauces or salt. With frozen fruit, it's important to check the labels to see what else might be added, like sugar.

Should I buy organic food?

If you can afford it, sure. But depending on your budget, it can be quite expensive. I'd rather people eat more fruits and vegetables that are nonorganic than eat a small amount of the organic variety. I eat lots of plants a week, and in general, most of it is organic, but I'm not obsessive about it. You will get more nutrients and polyphenols in organic plants, but another reason to eat them is the much lower levels of chemicals sprayed on them. Oats and oat bran are the main ones to buy organic if you eat them regularly, as they're sprayed to death with herbicides and pesticides to dry them out. If you're regularly eating berries, strawberries, and other things you can't peel, those are also good ones to replace with organic versions if you can. In summer, I eat tomatoes nearly every day, so I typically try to go organic for those, as I'd be accumulating quite a bit of pesticide otherwise. Organic foods are undoubtedly a better choice, and we want to support organic farming because farmers look after the soil as well as the plants. But the choice is not always clear-cut, and you need to balance it against what is most affordable for you.

Washing or peeling?

If you're worried about pesticides or bugs, it's usually best to wash your fruits and vegetables, although this won't remove all the chemicals (or microbes). Try not to peel them either if you can; for many plants, most of the nutrients, polyphenols, and fiber are on the outside layers. Good examples are kiwifruit and potatoes.

Is there a best time of day to eat my meals?

Yes, there are metabolically good and bad times to eat your meals. Generally, you should be eating meals at times you'd normally be active—during daylight hours, when your body's got all the hormones preparing it to do activity and exercise— not during rest times. Your body also needs time at night to recover as part of its circadian rhythm. Just like you need to sleep, your gut needs to rest. It's best to leave at least 12 hours without bothering your gut with food so it can repair itself and tidy up the gut lining. However, within those times, there's great individual variation, and these ideal eating patterns may change with age. They also typically change at menopause for women as hormone levels fluctuate. So don't assume that there's one particular pattern that suits everyone; instead, listen to your body and experiment to learn what works best for you. But remember, the fasting intervals and culture may be more important than the eating times, so don't let it mess up your vacation to the Mediterranean, where no one eats before 9pm.

Should I eat my food in a certain order?

My advice is not to worry about this too much. It's important to remember that as well as timings, most of our food choices and customs are cultural. If you go to other countries, you may well start your meal with some fresh mixed herbs or end with a really spicy drink, or have soup or curry for breakfast. We do know from our work at ZOE on blood sugar levels that there are several tactics to reduce excessive sugar peaks. Combining starchy foods with fats and fiber will slow the absorption and make the meal more satiating. There is also some emerging evidence that prioritizing high-fiber salads or other vegetables as starters 10 minutes or so before you have a carbohydrate-rich meal can help keep you fuller for longer and reduce the speed of absorption of the starchy food. This is why in France and Italy you are often served vegetables (antipasti and crudités) as a first course, often with an acidic vinaigrette. But this doesn't mean you should be dissecting a sandwich to eat its component parts, because that isn't practical, effective, or enjoyable. The most important point is to prioritize your meal as mainly plant-based with plenty of fiber and fewer highly refined carbohydrates.

Does my choice of vinegar matter?

Pick a vinegar you enjoy. It doesn't need to be expensive vinegar or even apple cider vinegar, as it seems to be the acidity level that is important for blood sugar. There is some recent evidence in small studies to suggest that you can blunt your body's blood sugar responses short-term by using vinegar on your salads before the main course.

Low-fat or full-fat?

I'm a big fan of full-fat natural foods. When manufacturers alter foods through industrial processes to make them low-fat or fat-free, it may give them a longer shelf life but strips away valuable vitamins, nutrients, and fatty acids like omega-3s. This process is similar to refining grains, where the end product is rich in carbohydrates but devoid of fats and many original nutrients. Despite popular belief in its health benefits, studies have not shown a clear advantage of low-fat milk over whole milk in terms of blood fat profiles or for weight control. And some research even suggests that full-fat milk may be better at improving beneficial blood fats.

Removing saturated fat content to produce low-fat dairy products eliminates other important nutritional elements that interact with our immune and metabolic systems and can influence aging—or cancer pathways. Although there are environmental and ethical considerations at play that one should consider, when consumed in moderation, full-fat dairy products do align with the dietary patterns of individuals with the healthiest blood profiles. That said, some people prefer low-fat milk, which is fine.

Are juices and smoothies healthy?

It's always better to eat your fruits and vegetables whole. Juices and smoothies are often marketed as healthy alternatives to sugary sodas and are included in many dietary recommendations as part of the daily fruit and vegetable intake. While fruit juices contain vitamins, nutrients, and polyphenols, they lack the beneficial fiber found in whole fruits. This absence of fiber means that the abundant sugars in the juice are more rapidly absorbed into your bloodstream, usually leading to spikes in blood sugar levels. A smoothie may retain more of the fruit's fiber when blended, but blending still alters the food matrix, leading to quicker sugar absorption than if the fruit were eaten whole. But adding whole vegetables to smoothies can be healthy if you wouldn't normally eat them.

Also important, drinking fruit juices over the long term has been associated with an increased risk of tooth decay, diabetes, and obesity, and with no health or mortality benefit, as opposed to regular whole fruit consumption, which is linked to reduced risks. This suggests that while fruit juices may not be quite as detrimental as sugary sodas, they can be seen as worse as they are wrongly portrayed as healthy. My advice would be to view them as an occasional treat.

Is it okay to eat meat and fish?

Processed meats have consistently been associated with negative health outcomes, including a higher risk of mortality, heart disease, and cancer. But we now understand that high-quality, unprocessed meats, especially those from animals with healthier lifestyles (like grass-fed and free-range), may not carry these risks and can be a source of beneficial nutrients like omega-3 fats, iron, zinc, and B vitamins. So, while highly processed meats aren't a great choice, eating a small amount of high-quality meat episodically has not been shown to be harmful.

While fish is often considered a healthier alternative to red meat, and I was told it would make me brainy, recent studies have not confirmed the strong benefits from fish consumption that were once assumed, such as significant prevention of heart disease or cancer. Also, given the associated environmental and sustainability issues—including overfishing and the ecological impact of fish farms—the recommendation to consume two to three portions of fish per week is now seen as unrealistic and likely harmful to the environment.

Interestingly, our individual chemical responses to consuming meat and fish can vary due to our differences in gut microbiota. While some people can handle meat consumption well, in others it could produce problematic chemicals that damage their blood vessels and heart. I follow a predominantly plant-based diet, but around once a month I might have a small amount of good-quality meat, and twice a month (usually when eating out) I have a good-quality piece of fish. But for me most of the time, as in this cookbook, plants are the stars of the show.

If I only eat plants, do I need extra protein?

Most people are fiber-deficient, not protein-deficient. There are plenty of proteins in most plants, especially in beans, legumes, whole grains, and mushrooms. Remember that protein is in nearly every food to some extent, and my favorite, legumes, are a key source of protein. If you don't eat dairy, meat, or fish, try to eat more nuts and legumes. Soybeans are also a fantastic source of protein, with a single portion of tofu providing 8g.

Do soybeans cause cancer?

Soybeans contain plant chemicals called isoflavones, which are a type of phytoestrogen. In the past, some worried that having these chemicals in your diet could increase certain types of estrogen-sensitive cancers, like breast cancer, for example. The science is very clear that this is not the case; in fact, diets with soy foods, including soybeans, are now thought to be protective for cancer and good for overall health.

Are raw vegetables better for you?

Vegetables are good for our health, whether they're raw or cooked. A few vegetables like beans, eggplant, and tubers can be toxic and are best not eaten raw, while the nutrients in many other vegetables are easier to absorb when they're cooked—beta-carotene in carrots and sweet potatoes or lycopene in tomatoes, for example. The key to eating vegetables is finding a way to eat them that works for you; raw is not necessarily better! In general, lightly cooked or steamed is best to preserve nutrients.

How can I pick the best vegan alternatives?

Although the field is moving fast and improving rapidly, you should focus on high-quality whole plants and plant combinations instead of trying to replace a meat-based food with something ultra-processed that is trying to mimic meat and often has little nutritional value. There are now good dairy-free alternatives for yogurt and milk, and I personally love adding blended soaked cashews or silken tofu to add creaminess to dishes. Try the Cashew Cream on page 268, in the Score Boosters chapter.

Should I worry about salt?

For the majority of people, restricting salt is not the only way to lower blood pressure or improve health. That said, some people (especially if you have African ancestry) are salt sensitive, so it is personalized. The food industry uses salt to make food hyperpalatable, so reducing salty UPFs is the best way to avoid this. Focusing on eating plenty of whole plants, rich in potassium and other protective phytonutrients, is the best way to look after your heart and control blood pressure. Studies show that adding potassium-rich foods to your diet has three times the benefit of reducing sodium in salt. It's also important to move regularly and drink mostly water, avoiding sugar-sweetened or energy drinks. A little salt makes food taste better and can encourage people to eat more plants and whole foods, which is the most important factor.

A Final Word

In my personal journey of applying the Food for Life science to the way I eat, what I've found most surprising is how much easier it is to regularly eat a vast array of vegetables than I would have imagined 10 years ago. Now, any vegetable cooked the right way is delicious. I used to loathe lentils, but I realize I was just eating them in a very bland way. Once I discovered the wonders of the spice drawer and how to combine legumes with other plants, a whole new world of possibilities opened up to me.

I still regularly encounter the challenge of how to balance eating to feel good while I'm traveling. What worked very well during Covid—when you knew exactly where you'd be for every meal because you were always at home—is a different kettle of fish today. Once again you have to be at a meeting at 8 in the morning, you don't know where you're going to be for lunch, and you haven't got any time to prepare a meal for the evening. This is where you have to change your tactics. I've learned to be much more flexible about how and when I eat my meals. For example, sometimes I eat my morning kefir with fruit and nuts for lunch or occasionally as an afternoon snack because I haven't had any fermented foods yet in my day.

Learning how to be flexible has also made me realize how important my overnight fast is for me. For years out of habit I ate my breakfast at 7:15 in the morning, and I didn't feel very good at all; now I know to eat it later in the day when I'm hungry—and when it will make me feel better. I also learned the importance of batch cooking and having a well-stocked pantry.

Don't be afraid to experiment and make mistakes—rest assured, I have made plenty. Just go for it with these recipes and enjoy the cooking journey with all of its surprises, as I have over the last few years. I'm generally a very messy cook in the kitchen because I like to explore different options and sometimes deviate from recipes. This mostly works out for me, but it can sometimes end in tears. My biggest weakness is the spice drawer, as I tend to over-flavor my meals. If a recipe says half a garlic clove or half a chile, I always double it. This usually works, but there have been some disasters, especially if we have a guest over who can't tolerate my level of spicing.

Other disasters I've encountered have involved my experiments with fermenting food. There have been times when I've been the only one who would drink my own kombucha, having left it too long and allowed it to become too sour. I've also had my turmeric-ginger water kefir explode on me and permanently stain my nice blue shirt as I opened it. Fermenting your own food at home is perfectly safe as long as you use clean jars, keep them out of strong sunlight, and "burp" your ferments regularly to avoid explosions, especially in hot weather and if they're not in the fridge. That said, perhaps it's best *not* to wear your favorite shirt in your early days of experimentation!

Why am I sharing these embarrassing kitchen setbacks with you? Because I want you to know that, wherever you are on the scale of cooking skills, this book is for you. Enjoy the challenges and the triumphs as they come, because the ultimate gift you're giving yourself and those around you is the joy of eating new, exciting home-cooked food that's delicious *and* fantastic for your gut microbiome. For every mishap in the kitchen, I've learned something new, shared a new favorite such as the Eggplant Schnitzel (page 164), and pleasantly surprised myself, family, or friends with updated recipes of old favorites like Juno's Lasagna and Asparagus–Pearl Barley Risotto (pages 203 and 166), which are now just as delicious as the originals and so much better for my health.

I encourage you to approach your journey with this book like a scientist. Explore what feels good for you and treat any disasters as good data for your own experiments. This cookbook brings the latest science and nutrition to your kitchen; now it's up to you to discover what makes you feel your best. Let me know how you get on.

Go boldly into your kitchen and—above all—enjoy!

Everyday Essentials

64 **Sauerkraut**

67 **Simple Kimchi**

68 **Seeded Soda Bread**

70 **Cinnamon-Pecan Granola**

73 **Nut-and-Seed Loaf**

The key to unlocking sustained health benefits through food is in forming lasting, positive daily habits that help you achieve all of the principles covered in this book. One fantastic day of gut-friendly eating won't move the needle long-term, nor will one very bland day—it's about general consistency over time.

You'll find these everyday essentials throughout the book because they're the high-scoring ZOE staples we can't go without. You'll be happy to hear that, yes, you *can* eat high-scoring gut-friendly breads that are quick and easy to make. And if you're anything like me, you'll soon discover there's nothing that isn't improved by a dollop of ferments like kimchi or sauerkraut, which is why you'll see them suggested as top-ups throughout the book. These all increase the plant and fiber count for your meals, which is a great bonus for your microbes, with each incremental increase of 5g of fiber delivering wonderful health benefits. If you start by incorporating these essentials into your daily meals, you'll be well on your way to feeling your best.

Sauerkraut

<5g
FIBER

2
PLANTS

Homemade ferments are cheaper than store-bought, and by making them yourself, you'll be sure of the ingredients and will know it wasn't pasteurized. One of the simplest ferments to start with is sauerkraut, which will work with additional vegetables and spices, as long as you remember to use a 2 percent salt solution (2g salt for every 3½ oz / 100g of shredded vegetables).

Method

1. Remove the tough outer leaves from the cabbage, reserving one and discarding the rest.

2. Thinly slice the cabbage, either by hand or using the slicer attachment on a food processor. Transfer to a bowl and scatter over the salt. Use your hands to massage the cabbage until it has reduced by almost half its size, softened significantly, and started to release some liquid—about 5 minutes. Stir in the caraway seeds.

3. Transfer to a clean 1½-pint / 750ml jar and press down firmly. Wash the reserved cabbage leaf and place this on top of the sauerkraut, pressing the shredded cabbage down so it is covered with brine (the cabbage leaf helps keep it submerged).

4. If the cabbage has not given off enough liquid at this point, mix ½ teaspoon salt in ½ cup / 125ml water and spoon enough brine into the jar to cover the cabbage by ½ inch / 1–2cm.

5. Push the cabbage leaf down and seal the jar with a lid. Allow to ferment for about 2 weeks at room temperature. Open the jar once a day to release the gas that has been given off during fermentation, also known as "burping." Start tasting after a week to test when it's ready; it should smell and taste pleasantly sour, although the longer you leave it, the more tangy it will become. Transfer to the fridge and enjoy liberally.

Preparation time: *20 minutes*

Ingredients *(Makes one 1½-pint / 750ml jar)*

1 white cabbage
 (1⅓ lb / 600g prepped weight)
2¼ tsp / 12g sea salt
 (or 2% of total weight)
1 tsp caraway seeds

Top-ups

Shredded red cabbage
Raw shredded beet
 (note that fermenting times will vary)
Spices *(experiment to your taste)*

EVERYDAY ESSENTIALS

<5g
FIBER

6
PLANTS

Simple Kimchi

Preparation time: *30 minutes, plus 1–2 hours soaking*

Ingredients *(Makes one 1½-pint / 750ml jar)*

1 napa cabbage,
  (about 10 oz / 300g prepped weight)
8 oz / 225g daikon, *trimmed*
4 green onions, *thinly sliced*
1 tbsp / 17g sea salt
  (or 3% of total weight of vegetables)
3–4 garlic cloves, *peeled*
1 (1-inch / 2.5cm) piece of ginger
1 tsp sugar
2 tbsp soy sauce
4 tbsp Korean red chile flakes
  (gochugaru)

Swap

Carrots for daikon *(or just use daikon as thin slices)*

The trick with fermented foods is to use them little and often. I now add about 2 tablespoons of kimchi anywhere I'd use chile sauce for an added ferment boost. This isn't a traditional kimchi, because it's vegan and doesn't include glutinous rice flour paste, but I hope the simplicity encourages you to give gut-friendly kimchi a go.

Method

1. Trim the core from the bottom of the cabbage and quarter it lengthwise. Weigh the trimmed cabbage, daikon, and green onions to calculate how much salt you need. Cut each cabbage quarter into thin (2-inch / 5cm) strips, then put the cabbage in a bowl and scatter over the salt. Massage with your hands until the cabbage begins to soften. Place a plate on top and weight it down with something heavy. Leave for 1–2 hours at room temperature.

2. When the cabbage is almost ready, make the paste. Blend the garlic, ginger, sugar, soy sauce, chile flakes, and 3 tablespoons of water in a food processor until you have a smooth paste. You may need to scrape down the sides of the bowl with a spatula. Keeping the paste in the food processor, attach the grating blade and grate the daikon into the paste.

3. Transfer the cabbage to a colander and rinse for a minute or so under cold water. Squeeze out any excess water and transfer to a large bowl. Add the paste and grated daikon to the bowl, followed by the green onions, and mix until the cabbage is thoroughly coated (if using your hands, a pair of rubber gloves is useful).

4. Transfer to a clean 1½-pint / 750ml jar and press down firmly until the vegetables are below the liquid, using excess cabbage leaves or weights (the core of the cabbage would work here) to help. Place the lid on top and leave to ferment for up to 5 days at room temperature, unsealing (burping) it daily to release any gas. Transfer to the fridge and use at every possible opportunity!

Seeded Soda Bread

<5g FIBER **8** PLANTS

This delicious recipe is essentially soda bread, but it's made with whole-grain rye flour and kefir. It's packed full of nuts and seeds and is especially easy to make. Because it freezes brilliantly, you'll always have a slice of bread ready to go.

Method

1. Preheat the oven to 350°F / 180°C and line a 2-lb / 900g loaf pan with parchment paper. If you don't have a loaf pan, line a baking sheet with parchment. Soak the prunes in ⅓ cup / 80ml boiling water.

2. Put the flour, flaxseed meal, baking soda, salt, seeds and nuts, and all but 1 tablespoon of the oats into a bowl and mix well. Add ¼ cup / 30g extra flour to the dough to make it easier to handle if you're making a round, free-form loaf.

3. Add the kefir to the prunes and their soaking liquid and blend with a handheld blender until smooth. Pour this into the bowl of dry ingredients, mixing very gently until you have a wet dough.

4. Transfer the mixture to the prepared loaf pan or baking sheet, sprinkle with the reserved oats, and flatten down slightly. Score a ¼-inch / ½cm-deep line down the middle of the loaf. Bake for 45 minutes, and 5 minutes before it's done, remove the pan from the oven and flip the loaf out. Return the loaf to the pan, now with the bottom side up, and place in the oven to get a nice even crust. Transfer to a wire rack to cool. This will keep for 5 days at room temperature and freezes well too; slice the loaf first so you can grab a slice or two from the freezer whenever you need it.

Preparation time: *10 minutes*
Cook time: *45 minutes*

Ingredients (Makes 20 slices)

2½ oz / 70g **soft pitted prunes** (about 10 prunes)
1¼ cups / 150g **whole-grain rye flour**
¾ cup / 85g **flaxseed meal**
1½ tsp **baking soda**
1½ tsp **sea salt**
1⅓ cups / 230g **mix of seeds and coarsely chopped nuts**
⅓ cup / 35g **old-fashioned rolled oats**
1¼ cups / 300ml **kefir**

Swap

Mixed seeds for nuts to make it nut-free

Cinnamon-Pecan Granola

5–10g FIBER **10** PLANTS

This granola makes a brilliant breakfast with kefir and fruit, but it's also a useful base for other recipes, like a crumble. Packed with nuts, it's great for your blood sugar response, and the oat bran is an easy win for getting more fiber into your diet. Don't move the pan after it comes out of the oven to ensure you get big, delicious clusters.

Method

1. Preheat the oven to 300°F / 150°C and line a 9 x 13-inch / 22 x 32cm baking sheet with parchment paper.

2. In a large bowl, mix together the dry ingredients. In a separate bowl, whisk together the almond butter, olive oil, and honey until combined. Add to the dry mixture and mix until everything is thoroughly coated.

3. Spread the granola mix out onto the lined baking sheet, pressing it into a single flat layer. Bake for 45 minutes, or until golden and crisp, checking halfway and turning if necessary to ensure it browns evenly.

4. When ready, remove from the oven and allow to cool completely on the baking sheet—this is really important to allow the granola to set so it can break into chunky pieces. Store in an airtight container for 2–3 weeks.

Preparation time: *10 minutes*
Cook time: *45 minutes*

Ingredients (Makes 10 portions)

½ cup / 60g slivered almonds
1 cup / 100g coarsely chopped pecans
1 cup / 120g oat bran
¾ cup / 85g mixed seeds
½ cup / 40g coconut flakes
2 tbsp chia seeds
2 tbsp flaxseed meal
2 tsp ground cinnamon
Pinch of salt
1 tbsp almond butter
5 tbsp / 100ml extra-virgin olive oil
4 tbsp honey

Swaps

Any nut butter for almond
Any nuts for pecans

EVERYDAY ESSENTIALS

5–10g **8**
FIBER PLANTS

Nut-and-Seed Loaf

Preparation time: *10 minutes, plus minimum 2 hours resting*
Cook time: *60 minutes*

Ingredients (Makes 10 slices)

½ cup / 85g sunflower seeds
½ cup / 80g pumpkin seeds
½ cup / 90g flaxseeds
¼ cup / 30g hazelnuts
¼ cup / 30g almonds
1½ cups / 145g rolled oats
2 tbsp chia seeds
¼ cup psyllium husks
   (*3 tbsp if using psyllium husk powder*)
Generous pinch of salt
3 tbsp extra-virgin olive oil

Top-up

Bruschetta toppings
   (*pages 120–123*)

Swaps

Sunflower seeds and pumpkin seeds for almonds and hazelnuts

With eight plants and packed with fiber, this is essentially my seed mix jar in loaf form. Based on Sarah Britton's (@mynewroots) famous recipe, this bread has been a ZOE community favorite for some time. It's especially delicious toasted and topped with avocado or as the basis for any of the bruschetta toppings (pages 120–123). Adjust the ratio and types of nuts and seeds to increase your daily plant count even more.

Method

1. Line a 2-lb / 900g loaf pan with parchment paper, then combine all the dry ingredients in a bowl.

2. In a jug, mix together the olive oil and 1½ cups / 350ml of water, then pour this into the bowl of dry ingredients, stirring to combine.

3. Immediately pour the mixture into the lined pan, pressing with the back of a spoon to flatten. Cover and leave at room temperature for at least 2 hours or, ideally, overnight.

4. When you are ready to bake, preheat the oven to 350°F / 180°C. Bake the loaf for 20 minutes, then remove the bread from the pan, place it upside down directly on the oven rack, and bake for a further 40 minutes.

5. Leave to cool completely before slicing, then store in an airtight container in the fridge or presliced in the freezer, ready for toasting.

Mornings

76 Tim's Break-fast Bowl
78 Herby Green-Pea Pancakes
81 Raspberry-Lemon Pancakes
82 Green Shakshuka
84 Black Bean Avocado Toast
87 Spicy Gochujang Beans
88 Probiotic Bircher Muesli
91 Sauerkraut Frittata
92 Spiced Pear Oatmeal
94 Miso-Spinach Eggs
96 Corn Fritters

At night the gut barrier repairs itself as part of its circadian rhythm, and the gut microbiome is an essential part of this process. By giving it time to rest and rejuvenate, you're supporting this natural rhythm, which means that how and when you break your overnight fast will have a big impact on how you feel for the rest of the day. Our research at ZOE has revealed that around a quarter of people experience a significant blood sugar dip after a sugary breakfast, leading to increased hunger later in the day. We've also found that your blood sugar responses to your first meal vary based on how well you've slept.

We all process and absorb food differently. For some, a substantial breakfast will be beneficial, while for others—myself included—skipping it, delaying it, or eating lightly is best. That's why this chapter is named "Mornings" rather than "Breakfast," in case you're someone who likes to give your gut bacteria a longer break. We've included light bites as well as more substantial dishes to help you start your day in the best way for *you*.

Tim's Break-fast Bowl

5–10g FIBER   **7** PLANTS

I'm often asked about my go-to breakfast, and here it is. With plenty of plants and a probiotic boost from the kefir, it's my favorite way to start the day. Treat the ingredients as a guide and use whatever fruit, nuts, and seeds you have. Fresh berries aren't always in season, so I typically use frozen ones, which delivers plenty of flavor and some of those rainbow colors while still retaining the essential polyphenols and nutrients.

Method

Mix the Greek yogurt and kefir in a bowl and top with the remaining ingredients.

Preparation time: *5 minutes*

Ingredients (Serves 1–2)

½ cup / 125g Greek yogurt
⅓ cup / 80ml kefir
1⅓ cups / 200g mix of fruit, *defrosted if frozen*
2 tbsp Seed Mix Sprinkle (*page 263*)
1 tbsp almonds
1 tbsp walnuts
1 tbsp pecans

Top-ups

Nut butter
Cinnamon-Pecan Granola (*page 70*)

Swaps

Plant-based yogurt and kefir alternatives
Extra seeds for nuts

Herby Green-Pea Pancakes

5–10g FIBER   **6** PLANTS

That bag of peas in the back of your freezer finally gets its time to shine in these delicious savory pancakes, adding protein and fiber to your morning meal. Frozen peas typically have more vitamin C than fresh, while the cottage cheese adds extra protein, slowing your blood sugar response. Top with a poached egg for a satisfying brunch, or use any leftover batter to make a great light lunch, served with a side salad.

Method

1. Put the cottage cheese and egg into a blender and blend until smooth. Add most of the peas and blend again until almost smooth but retaining some texture.

2. Pour the mixture into a bowl and stir in the flour, lemon zest, herbs, green onions, the remaining peas, and a pinch of salt and pepper. Mix until combined—if the batter seems too thick, add up to 3 tablespoons of water to reach a spoonable consistency.

3. Heat the olive oil in a large nonstick frying pan over medium heat. When hot, drop 2 generous spoonfuls of the mixture into the pan to form pancakes. Cook for 2 minutes on each side, until golden. Repeat with the remaining batter.

Preparation time: *15 minutes*
Cook time: *5 minutes*

Ingredients *(Makes 4 pancakes)*

½ cup / 120g cottage cheese
1 medium egg
1½ cups / 200g frozen peas
⅓ cup / 50g whole-grain spelt flour
Zest of 1 lemon
1½ cups / 60g mix of green herbs *(e.g., mint, basil), coarsely chopped*
4 green onions, *thinly sliced*
1 tbsp extra-virgin olive oil
Salt and black pepper

Top-ups

Yogurt
Boiled or poached egg
Chile oil

Swaps

Silken tofu for cottage cheese
Whole-wheat flour for spelt flour
Flax egg for egg

5–10g
FIBER

3
PLANTS

Raspberry-Lemon Pancakes

Preparation time: *8 minutes*
Cook time: *8 minutes*

This recipe takes its sweetness from the raspberries, which also happen to be one of the highest-fiber fruits—frozen ones are perfect to use when fresh are out of season. Add a seed mix to the batter to increase the plant count, and the protein from the cottage cheese will moderate your blood sugar response.

Ingredients (Serves 2)

1¼ cups / 150g raspberries
⅔ cup / 60g old-fashioned rolled oats
½ cup / 120g cottage cheese
1 medium egg
Zest of 1 lemon
¼ tsp baking powder
Pinch of salt
2 tsp extra-virgin olive oil, plus more as needed
¼ cup Greek yogurt, *to serve*

Method

1. Put half of the raspberries and 1 tablespoon of water into a small saucepan and mash with a fork. Place over low heat and simmer for 2–3 minutes, stirring, until you have a thick compote.

2. Put the oats into a blender or food processor and process to a flour-like consistency. Add the cottage cheese, egg, lemon zest, baking powder, salt, and 1 tablespoon of water. Process until smooth, scraping down the sides as you go. The batter should be thick but pourable. Pour into a bowl and stir in the remaining raspberries.

3. Heat the olive oil in a large nonstick frying pan over medium heat and drop spoonfuls of the mixture into the pan to form 6 small pancakes. Fry for 2 to 4 minutes on each side. You may need to do this in batches—use a little extra oil if so.

4. When ready, serve the pancakes stacked on a plate with the Greek yogurt and raspberry compote.

Top-ups

Cinnamon-Pecan Granola *(page 70)*
Seed Mix Sprinkle *(page 263)*
Kefir

Swaps

Plant-based yogurt alternative
Blueberries for raspberries

Green Shakshuka

10–15g FIBER **7** PLANTS

The beans in this dish make it a hearty and satisfying meal to break your fast, and the spices count toward your 30 plants too. You can use eggs or tofu: they're both great sources of micronutrients. The squeeze of lime at the end with its vitamin C content helps you absorb the plant iron from the leafy greens. Bonus tip: chopping your garlic 10 minutes before cooking will increase its allicin content, and its potential health benefits.

Method

1. Heat the olive oil in a large frying pan over medium heat, add the leek, and sauté for 3 minutes, until softened. Add the garlic, cumin seeds, chile flakes, and a pinch of salt and cook for 30 seconds more.

2. Turn the heat to high and add the kale, cranberry beans and their liquid, the Boosting Bouillon, and 7 tbsp / 100ml water. Boil rapidly for 3 minutes, stirring once or twice, until the kale has wilted and the sauce has thickened and reduced. Season to taste.

3. Make four wells in the center of the mixture and crack an egg into each one. Reduce the heat to medium, cover the pan with a lid or sheet of foil, and cook until the whites are set but the yolks are still runny, 4–5 minutes. Scatter over the cilantro and serve with the lime wedges and some freshly ground black pepper.

Preparation time: *8 minutes*
Cook time: *12 minutes*

Ingredients (Serves 2)

2 tbsp extra-virgin olive oil
1 leek, *thinly sliced*
2 garlic cloves, *coarsely chopped*
1 tbsp cumin seeds
½ tsp chile flakes
6 cups / 100g shredded kale
1 (14-oz / 400g) can cranberry beans and their liquid
1½ tbsp Boosting Bouillon *(page 264)*
4 medium eggs
⅓ cup / 15g cilantro, *coarsely chopped*
Salt and black pepper
Lime wedges, *to serve*

Top-ups

Kefir
Seed Mix Sprinkle *(page 263)*
Fresh chile, chopped or sliced

Swaps

Cubed smoked tofu for eggs
Any beans for cranberry beans
Miso for Boosting Bouillon

Black Bean Avocado Toast

10–15g **6**
FIBER PLANTS

If there are fewer than four of you eating, you'll be glad of the extra come tomorrow. The black bean and avocado topping is a bigger batch than you need, and it'll keep for up to 3 days in the fridge. Lime juice preserves the vibrant green color and flavor of the avocado—a high-fiber favorite. The black beans are also packed with polyphenols and fiber, so they're fantastic for your gut health. Enjoy this for breakfast or lunch, or as a healthy, go-to snack.

Method

1. Cut each avocado in half, scoop out the flesh, and chop it coarsely, then add the lime zest and juice and mix well. Do this as soon as possible to prevent the avocado from browning.

2. In a separate bowl, mash half of the black beans until they are mostly broken down. Add the remaining beans, the cilantro, pumpkin seeds, chile flakes (if using), olive oil, and avocado to the bowl and mix until well combined. Season with salt and pepper.

3. Slice and toast the bread and then top with the black bean and avocado mixture. Any remaining topping will keep in the fridge for up to 3 days—simply make sure it is covered with some wax paper or kept in a lidded container.

Preparation time: *15 minutes*

Ingredients (Serves 4)

3 ripe avocados
Zest of 2 limes and juice of 1
1 (14-oz / 400g) can black beans,
  drained and rinsed
⅓ cup / 15g cilantro,
  finely chopped
2 tbsp pumpkin seeds
1 tsp chile flakes (optional)
1 tbsp extra-virgin olive oil
Salt and black pepper
Seeded Soda Bread (page 68)

Top-ups

Sumac
Kimchi

Swaps

Mint for cilantro
Any seeds for pumpkin

<5g FIBER   **7** PLANTS

Spicy Gochujang Beans

Preparation time: *10 minutes*
Cook time: *12 minutes*

Ingredients (Serves 2)

1 tbsp extra-virgin olive oil
1 small onion, *finely chopped*
5 oz / 150g cremini mushrooms, *sliced*
1 garlic clove, *finely chopped*
10 cherry tomatoes, *halved*
2 tsp gochujang (*or to taste*)
2 tbsp Boosting Bouillon (*page 264*)
1 (14-oz / 400g) can lima beans and their liquid
4½ cups / 90g fresh spinach
Salt and black pepper
Seeded Soda Bread (*page 68*) **or sourdough bread**

Top-ups

Poached or soft-boiled egg
Fresh chile

Swap

Any white beans for lima beans

Beans take center stage here as a rich source of protein and fiber. If you're ever stuck on what to cook, having a can of beans in your pantry means you're only minutes away from a delicious, flexible meal for you and your microbes. This is a great one for batch cooking, so do think of doubling up and freezing a portion. It also keeps in the fridge for up to 4 days.

Method

1. Heat the oil in a frying pan over medium heat, add the onion and mushrooms, and sauté for 5 minutes, stirring occasionally, until softened. Stir in the garlic and cook for 30 seconds more.

2. Add the tomatoes, gochujang, Boosting Bouillon, and beans and their liquid to the pan. Mix well and simmer for 4–5 minutes, until it has thickened to your liking.

3. Remove from the heat and stir the spinach into the mixture until it is almost fully wilted but still holding some of its shape and texture. Season with salt and pepper and serve with the bread (toasted if you like).

Probiotic Bircher Muesli

5–10g FIBER **5** PLANTS

Pack in as many seeds and nuts as you like in this overnight muesli to get closer to your 30-plants-a-week total. The kefir has around 7 times as many bacteria strains as yogurt, and the protein will mean you start your day satisfied. This recipe will keep for up to 3 days in the fridge, so double the recipe to get ahead for the week, adding additional kefir to thin as needed.

Method

1. Measure all the ingredients into a bowl, mix to combine, then cover and leave in the fridge for at least 2 hours or overnight.

2. Thin with additional milk or kefir if needed.

Preparation time: *8 minutes*

Ingredients (Serves 1–2)

1 apple, *coarsely grated*
½ cup / 125ml kefir
¼ cup / 60ml milk of choice *(or extra kefir), plus extra to serve*
2 tbsp Greek yogurt
1 tsp ground cinnamon
½ to ⅔ cup / 60g rolled oats
2 tbsp Seed Mix Sprinkle *(page 263)*

Top-ups

Berries
Sweet Crispy Pulses and Grains *(page 267)*
Nuts

Swaps

Pear for apple
1 recipe Cashew Cream *(page 268)* **for kefir, milk, and yogurt**

<5g
FIBER

8
PLANTS

Sauerkraut Frittata

Preparation time: *10 minutes*
Cook time: *18 minutes*

Ingredients (Serves 4)

2 tbsp extra-virgin olive oil
1 onion, *finely chopped*
¾ cup / 30g finely chopped parsley
½ tsp paprika
2–3 roasted red peppers from a jar, *finely chopped*
5 medium eggs
2 tbsp Seed Mix Sprinkle *(page 263)*
3 tbsp Sauerkraut, *plus extra to serve (page 64)*
Salt and black pepper

Top-ups

Arugula
Kimchi

Swaps

Dill for parsley
Harissa or chile flakes for paprika

If you're pressed for time in the morning, this is a great recipe to make in advance. The generous amount of herbs in this dish gives it a really robust flavor, and it's a great base to use with whatever additional ingredients you have on hand, reducing food waste. Cooking the sauerkraut will destroy the live bacteria, so sprinkle some more on top at the very end too.

Method

1. Heat the olive oil in a medium nonstick frying pan over low heat and sauté the onion for 10 minutes, until soft and starting to caramelize.

2. Transfer to a bowl (leaving as much oil as possible in the pan) and add the parsley, paprika, roasted red peppers, eggs, seeds, and a pinch of salt and pepper. Whisk until combined.

3. Preheat your broiler to its highest setting and return the pan to medium heat. Pour the egg mixture into the pan (there should be enough residual oil from the onions) and cook for 4 minutes, or until the edges are starting to set.

4. Scatter the sauerkraut all over the top of the frittata and place under the broiler for 3 minutes, until the frittata is fully set. Serve hot or cold, sprinkled with a little extra sauerkraut. The frittata will keep in the fridge for up to 2 days.

Spiced Pear Oatmeal

15–20g FIBER **7** PLANTS

The inclusion of oat bran, which is the outer layer of the husked oat kernel, is key to this recipe's impressive fiber count. With more than three times more fiber than regular rolled oats, it's a real feast for your gut microbiome. Adding the healthy fats from the nut butter will help slow the absorption of sugar and make the oatmeal extra creamy.

Method

1. Put the oats, milk, cinnamon, and salt into a small nonstick saucepan over medium heat and cook for 5–6 minutes, stirring occasionally, until the oats have softened slightly.

2. Add the oat bran and seeds and cook for 3 minutes longer, stirring all the time. It will thicken very quickly. Add a little more milk, to taste. Serve in a bowl topped with the sliced pear and nut butter.

Preparation time: *3 minutes*
Cook time: *8 minutes*

Ingredients *(Serves 1–2)*

⅓ **cup / 30g rolled oats**
1½ **cups / 375ml milk of choice, plus more to serve**
½ **tsp ground cinnamon**
Pinch of salt
¼ **cup / 30g oat bran**
3½ **tbsp Seed Mix Sprinkle** *(page 263)*
1 small pear, *sliced*
1 tbsp unsweetened nut butter

Top-ups

Berries
Kefir
Cinnamon-Pecan Granola *(page 70)*

Swap

Apple for pear

Miso-Spinach Eggs

<5g FIBER **4** PLANTS

Egg yolks have a lot of micronutrients, so be sure not to skip them. If you're worried about cholesterol, rest assured that the idea you need to limit eggs for your heart is a myth. Starting with a breakfast full of fat and protein like this helps stabilize your blood sugar so you can keep going until lunch. This tastes delicious on Seeded Soda Bread.

Method

1. Whisk the eggs and miso together until combined and set aside. Heat the olive oil in a nonstick frying pan over medium heat, add the spinach, and cook for 1 minute, stirring, until almost completely wilted. Transfer to a bowl and keep warm.

2. Return the frying pan to low heat and add the eggs. Stir continuously for 2 minutes, until scrambled. Remove from the heat and stir in the spinach. Season with pepper (there will already be sufficient saltiness from the miso).

3. Scatter over the mixed seeds and green onion and serve.

Preparation time: *5 minutes*
Cook time: *3 minutes*

Ingredients (Serves 1)

2 medium eggs
1 tsp miso
1 tsp extra-virgin olive oil
4 cups / 80g fresh spinach
1 tbsp Seed Mix Sprinkle *(page 263)*
1 green onion, *finely chopped*
Black pepper

Top-ups

Seeded Soda Bread *(page 68)*
Kimchi

Swap

Gochujang for miso

Corn Fritters

<5g FIBER   **9** PLANTS

This satisfying, Australia-influenced recipe is packed full of plants and protein. It also makes great use of canned vegetables, which I'm a huge fan of. Canned vegetables are often just as nutritious, last much longer, and are an affordable way to increase your plant intake. The recipe for these fritters is slightly more involved than others in this chapter, so they will suit a more relaxed, weekend-style brunch.

Method

1. Preheat the oven to 425°F / 220°C. Lay the tomatoes cut-side down on a baking sheet lined with parchment paper, drizzle with 1 tablespoon of the olive oil, season, and roast for 20 minutes.

2. In a bowl, mix the tofu and rye flour together until you have a smooth paste. Add the halloumi, corn, cilantro, chile, seed mix, lime zest and juice, 1 tablespoon of olive oil, and a pinch each of salt and pepper and mix to combine. Use your hands to shape the mixture into 8 fritters, each roughly ½ inch / 1cm thick. It helps if you dampen your hands with a little water first.

3. Heat the remaining tablespoon of oil in a large nonstick frying pan over medium heat, and when hot, fry 4 of the fritters for 3–4 minutes on each side, until golden and crispy. When ready, set aside on a plate lined with paper towels and keep warm. Repeat with the remaining fritters, adding a little more oil if necessary.

4. Reduce the heat to low and add the spinach to the pan. Cook for 1 minute, stirring all the time, until wilted. Season with salt and pepper. Serve two fritters per person, with a couple of tomatoes on the side and a generous pile of wilted spinach.

Preparation time: *2 minutes*
Cook time: *30 minutes*

Ingredients (Serves 4)

4 tomatoes, *halved*
3 tbsp extra-virgin olive oil
3½ oz / 100g silken tofu
⅓ cup / 40g whole-grain rye flour
3½ oz / 100g halloumi, *coarsely grated*
1 cup / 200g canned corn, *drained (5¾ oz / 160g drained weight)*
¾ cup / 30g chopped cilantro
1 small fresh red chile, *finely chopped*
1 tsp Seed Mix Sprinkle (page 263)
Zest and juice of 1 lime
8 oz / 240g spinach
Salt and black pepper

Top-ups

Kefir Dressing (page 271)
Kimchi

Swaps

Firm tofu for halloumi

15-Minute Meals

- 100 **Creamy Kale Pasta**
- 103 **Smashed Pea Bowl**
- 104 **Hazelnut Gremolata–Corn Salad**
- 106 **Beans Three Ways**
  - **Tahini-Miso Beans**
  - **Cacio e Pepe Chickpeas**
  - **Artichoke Lima Beans**
- 110 **Green Goddess Chickpea Sandwich**
- 113 **Kale and Cashew Soup**
- 114 **Spinach Wraps with Roasted Pepper**
- 116 **Instant Noodles**
- 119 **Kefir Curried Chickpeas**
- 120 **Seeded Bruschetta Three Ways**
  - **Harissa Mushrooms**
  - **Tricolore**
  - **Kimchi Broccolini**

The most common request from our ZOE community is for inspiration for quick meals, particularly lunches. Two of the biggest limitations to eating better are time and money; when we're short on either, it's all too tempting to grab the closest, cheapest thing, which is often an ultra-processed food (UPF) or a bland staple. And I was no different: my go-to lunch as a junior doctor was a store-bought sandwich and a bag of chips.

Studies have shown that eating UPFs regularly can lead to a host of poor health outcomes, so when you're in the middle of a busy day, it's helpful to have a few tasty recipes up your sleeve that can be rustled up quickly. Several in this chapter are twists on classic lunchtime staples; for example, did you know you can make your own gut-friendly wrap in mere minutes? Precooked packages of lentils and cans of beans are your time-saving friends here. A quick lunch can soon become a moment of pleasure in the middle of your day.

Creamy Kale Pasta

10–15g FIBER   **4** PLANTS

A good pasta can be so satisfying, and this recipe improves the nutritional value by adding our beloved fiber-packed beans, which also make the sauce creamy and delicious. Including extra seeds on top will bring a delightful crunch, plus added fiber, good fats, and protein.

Method

1. Bring two saucepans of salted water to a boil. Put the pasta in one and cook for 8–10 minutes, until al dente.

2. Put the kale and garlic in the other saucepan and blanch for 3 minutes. When ready, drain and add to a blender with the lemon juice and Boosting Bouillon.

3. Pour the beans into a sieve set over a bowl, keeping the liquid from the can. Add a quarter of the beans to the blender along with the reserved liquid and blend until totally smooth.

4. When the pasta is ready, drain it, reserving 2 tablespoons of the cooking water. Return the pasta to the pan along with the remaining beans, reserved cooking water, and the blended sauce. Heat through for a minute or so, taste and season if necessary, and serve.

Preparation time: *5 minutes*
Cook time: *10 minutes*

Ingredients (Serves 2)

3 oz / 90g whole-wheat pasta
3½ oz / 100g kale,
   stalks removed and thinly sliced
1 garlic clove
Juice of 1 lemon
2 tbsp Boosting Bouillon
   (page 264)
1 (14-oz / 400g) can cannellini beans and their liquid
Salt and black pepper

Top-ups

Sauerkraut *(page 64)*
Seed Mix Sprinkle *(page 263)*

Swap

Nutritional yeast or Parmesan for Boosting Bouillon

10–15g
FIBER

8
PLANTS

Smashed Pea Bowl

Preparation time: *5 minutes*
Cook time: *10 minutes*

Ingredients (Serves 2)

10 cherry tomatoes
3½ oz / 100g broccolini
1 tbsp extra-virgin olive oil
Salt and black pepper

For the smashed pea dip

1⅓ cups / 185g frozen peas
2 green onions,
   coarsely chopped
Small handful each mint
   and cilantro leaves
1 small fresh green chile,
   chopped
1 preserved lemon (*optional*)
Juice of 1 lemon
3 tbsp extra-virgin olive oil

¾ cup / 140g cooked lentils

Top-ups

Sauerkraut (*page 64*)
Seed Mix Sprinkle (*page 263*)

Swap

Any vegetable for topping

The frozen peas in this dish are packed with vitamin C and provide a great source of protein. It's also a highly adaptable recipe: you can enjoy it as is or use it as a base for other favorite toppings, such as roasted vegetables, lentils, canned beans, or feta cheese. Also try dipping crudités into the peas for a delicious snack—the options are endless.

Method

1. Preheat the oven to 425°F / 220°C. Put the tomatoes and broccolini into a small roasting dish, season with salt and pepper, and drizzle the olive oil on top. Roast for 10 minutes.

2. Cover the peas with boiling water and leave for 1 minute to defrost. Drain and add to a blender with the green onions, herbs, green chile, preserved lemon (if using), lemon juice, and olive oil. Season and blend until smooth.

3. Divide the smashed peas between two plates and top with the cooked lentils and roasted vegetables.

Hazelnut Gremolata–Corn Salad

5–10g FIBER   **8** PLANTS

This dish takes less than 15 minutes to prepare but feels like so much more than the sum of its parts, with its citrusy gremolata and slivers of corn sliced from the cob. The hazelnuts add protein and fiber, and the lemon juice adds a welcome zing to balance the sweetness, making it a satisfying and sophisticated meal ready in no time at all.

Method

1. Fill a large saucepan with water and add a pinch of salt; bring to a boil. Reduce the heat to medium, add the corn cobs, and cook for 5 minutes.

2. Meanwhile, put the parsley, hazelnuts, lemon zest, half the lemon juice, the garlic, and olive oil in a food processor with a pinch of salt and pepper. Blend until finely chopped.

3. Drain the corn and carefully slice the kernels from the cobs using a sharp knife. Place in a large bowl with the arugula and gremolata, tossing to combine. Top with the seed mix, squeeze over a little more lemon juice to taste, and serve.

Preparation time: *10 minutes*
Cook time: *5 minutes*

Ingredients *(Serves 2)*

- 3 large ears corn, shucked
- ⅔ cup / 25g coarsely chopped parsley
- ⅓–½ cup / 50g blanched hazelnuts
- Zest and juice of ½ lemon
- ½ garlic clove, *finely grated*
- 3 tbsp extra-virgin olive oil
- 1 cup / 20g arugula
- 2 tbsp Seed Mix Sprinkle *(page 263)*
- Salt and black pepper

Top-ups

- Sauerkraut *(page 64)*
- Chile oil

Swaps

- Canned corn for fresh
- Sunflower seeds for hazelnuts

Beans Three Ways

The following recipes are all variations on one of my favorite ingredients, beans. Depending on what you eat them with, these recipes will serve 1–2 people, but I'm always happy to have leftovers, as they make a great lunch the next day.

Tahini-Miso Beans

5–10g FIBER   **6** PLANTS

In those moments when you don't have time to cook or when there's nothing in the fridge, a can of beans can save the day. Packed with plant protein and fiber, the miso adds a delicious umami flavor, and the tahini makes these beans deliciously creamy. Add any toppings you like, such as tomatoes, cucumber, cilantro, or lime juice.

Preparation time: *5 minutes*
Cook time: *7 minutes*

Ingredients (Serves 1–2)

1 tbsp extra-virgin olive oil
1 shallot, *finely chopped*
1 garlic clove, *finely chopped*
1 (14-oz / 400g) can cannellini beans and their liquid
1 tsp miso
1 tbsp tahini
2 tbsp kimchi
Salt and black pepper

Top-ups

Seed Mix Sprinkle (*page 263*)
Cilantro

Swaps

Any white beans for cannellini
Small onion for shallot

Method

1. Heat the olive oil in a medium frying pan over medium heat and sauté the shallot for 2 minutes, until softened and turning golden. Add the garlic and cook for 30 seconds longer.

2. Pour in the beans and their liquid and simmer for 3 minutes, until the liquid has reduced slightly, thickened, and become creamy.

3. Turn off the heat and stir in the miso and tahini. This will thicken the beans, so add a splash of water if necessary. Season with salt and pepper and serve topped with the kimchi.

Cacio e Pepe Chickpeas

5–10g FIBER **2** PLANTS

15-MINUTE MEALS

Inspired by Yotam Ottolenghi's dish of a similar name, we've taken the classic Roman pasta dish and served it with chickpeas in place of the pasta. This creates a fiber-packed feast for you and your gut microbes. Including a fermented cheese like Parmesan has an added probiotic benefit.

Method

1. Heat the olive oil in a medium frying pan over medium heat and sauté the garlic and 1 teaspoon of the black pepper together for 30–40 seconds, until aromatic.

2. Pour in the chickpeas and their liquid and simmer everything together for 3 minutes, until the sauce has thickened slightly.

3. Remove from the heat and stir in the cheese until melted. Add a dash of water if necessary to give the sauce a creamy consistency.

4. Season with a pinch of salt and serve with more black pepper.

Preparation time: *3 minutes*
Cook time: *5 minutes*

Ingredients (Serves 1–2)

1 tbsp extra-virgin olive oil
1 garlic clove, *finely chopped*
1 (14-oz / 400g) can chickpeas and their liquid
1 cup / 30g grated Parmesan or pecorino (*or ideally a mixture of both*)
Salt and black pepper

Top-ups

Fried sage
Sauerkraut (*page 64*)
Chile flakes

Swaps

Any white beans for chickpeas
2 tbsp nutritional yeast for Parmesan

10–15g **6**
FIBER PLANTS

Artichoke Lima Beans

Preparation time: *7 minutes*
Cook time: *7 minutes*

Ingredients *(Serves 1–2)*

1 tbsp extra-virgin olive oil
1 **shallot,** *finely chopped*
1 **garlic clove,** *chopped*
1 **(14-oz / 400g) can lima beans and their liquid**
½ **(10-oz / 285g) jar artichokes,** *drained and coarsely chopped*
2 **sun-dried tomatoes,** *thinly sliced*
2½ **cups / 50g lightly packed spinach**
Juice of 1 lemon

Top-ups

Sourdough toast
Sauerkraut *(page 64)*
Nut Crumb *(page 262)*

Swaps

Any white beans for lima beans
Frozen spinach for fresh

This flavorsome dish is packed full of prebiotics from the lima beans and the artichokes. Cooking the spinach with garlic and shallot and adding vitamin C from the lemon juice helps your body absorb the iron. I always have frozen spinach in my freezer—it retains all the essential nutrients; you can sub it here for the fresh if you like.

Method

1. Heat the oil in a frying pan over medium heat, add the shallot, and sauté for 2 minutes, until turning golden. Add the garlic and cook for 20 seconds more.

2. Pour in the lima beans and their liquid, the artichokes, sun-dried tomatoes, spinach, and lemon juice. Stir to combine and simmer for 2–3 minutes, until the liquid has reduced and thickened slightly (it will take a little longer if you're using frozen spinach). Serve with a drizzle of olive oil.

Green Goddess Chickpea Sandwich

10–15g FIBER **7** PLANTS

In terms of convenience, sandwiches are hard to beat when you're on the go, but most ready-made options are ultra-processed. This one is full of fiber from the chickpeas and healthy fats from the avocado, which help moderate your blood sugar response. You'll also be well on your way to 30 plants a week with the mix of herbs, and the kefir provides probiotics and creaminess. The sauce also makes a great salad dressing, and any leftover chickpea mix a lovely breakfast or lunch.

Method

1. Put the avocado, kefir, lemon juice, garlic, and vinegar into a blender with a pinch of salt and pepper and blend until smooth.

2. Put the chickpeas into a bowl and pour over the avocado mixture. Mash together until combined, but still chunky. Stir in the green onions and herbs.

3. Divide the chickpeas between two pieces of toast and top with the tomatoes and a pinch of salt and pepper. Top with the remaining toast slices to create two sandwiches.

Preparation time: *10 minutes*

Ingredients (Serves 2)

1 avocado
3 tbsp kefir
Juice of 1 lemon
1 garlic clove
1 tsp apple cider vinegar
1 (14-oz / 400g) can chickpeas, *drained*
2 green onions, *thinly sliced*
1 tbsp each of coarsely chopped parsley and dill
4 slices sourdough bread, *toasted*
1 tomato, *sliced into 4*
Salt and black pepper

Top-ups

Kimchi
Arugula
Sprouts

Swaps

Any vinegar for apple cider vinegar
Any white beans for chickpeas

<5g   **6**
FIBER   PLANTS

Kale and Cashew Soup

Preparation time: *3 minutes*
Cook time: *8 minutes*

Ingredients (Serves 4)

½ cup / 65g **cashews**
1 (1-oz / 25g) piece of **ginger**
    (no need to peel), coarsely chopped
1 small fresh **red chile,** *stemmed*
1½ tbsp **miso**
7 oz / 200g (a large bunch) **kale,** *stemmed and shredded*
4 tbsp **kimchi**
Salt and black pepper

Top-ups

Kimchi
Savory Crispy Pulses and Grains
    (page 267)
Seed Mix Sprinkle *(page 263)*

Swap

Spinach for kale

The base of this delicious soup, made from cashews, ginger, chile, and miso, creates a bold flavor in minimal time. The ginger has a fantastic heat that will warm you from the inside out, while the kimchi adds a nice crunch and probiotic boost. Save any leftovers for tomorrow's lunch.

Method

1. Put the cashews, ginger, chile, and miso into a high-powered blender with 1 cup / 250ml water and blend until totally smooth to create a stock.

2. In a saucepan, bring 3⅓ cups / 800ml water to a boil. Add the stock and then the kale and mix to combine.

3. Simmer over medium heat for 5 minutes, until the kale has softened but is still vibrant green. Use a handheld blender to partially blend the soup—you want to keep some of the texture from the kale. Season and serve topped with the kimchi.

Spinach Wraps with Roasted Pepper

10–15g FIBER   **9** PLANTS

I used to buy ready-made wraps on the go, thinking they were healthy, but they're often not as healthy as they seem. They can have added chemicals to extend their shelf life, putting them firmly in the ultra-processed food category. It's surprisingly quick and easy to make a much healthier and tastier wrap at home to take with you. I love the pepper-cheese combo here, but this is really an invitation to build from the wrap base and create your own favorites.

Method

1. Put the spinach, chickpea flour, and flaxseed meal in a blender with 5 tablespoons of water and a pinch of salt and pepper. Blend until smooth.

2. Place a nonstick frying pan over medium-low heat and add the olive oil. When hot, pour in the spinach batter, spread out with a spatula to cover the base of the pan, and cook for 2 minutes. Carefully flip over and cook for 1 minute longer, then transfer to a plate lined with paper towels to absorb any excess oil.

3. Spread the filling ingredients onto the wrap, drizzle the Kimchi Dressing all over, and roll up tightly. Enjoy immediately or wrap in some wax paper or foil for later.

15-MINUTE MEALS

Preparation time: *10 minutes*
Cook time: *3 minutes*

Ingredients (Serves 1)

For the wrap

1½ cups / 30g spinach
Scant ½ cup / 50g chickpea flour
1 tbsp flaxseed meal
Salt and black pepper
1 tsp extra-virgin olive oil,
   for frying

For the filling

1½ cups / 30g spinach
1 roasted red pepper from a jar,
   coarsely chopped
2 tbsp crumbled feta cheese
2 tbsp Sauerkraut *(page 64)*
1 tbsp Seed Mix Sprinkle
   (page 263)
1 tbsp Kimchi Dressing
   (page 270)

Top-ups

Pumpkin seeds
Sandwich filling of your choice

Swap

Whole-grain flour for chickpea

Instant Noodles

5–10g FIBER **7** PLANTS

This recipe is one that you can—and should—adapt to your taste buds and the contents of your vegetable drawer. It's important to use a canning jar, as they're built to withstand high heat. A 1-pint / 500ml jar will take 7 oz / 200g of thinly sliced vegetables, whichever combination you use. For the noodles, experiment with what you have available—edamame noodles are sometimes called "soybean noodles," and are packed with plant protein and fiber.

Method

1. Thinly slice the carrot, pepper, radishes, and green onions.

2. Spoon the ginger, miso, soy sauce, and kimchi and its brine into a 1-pint / 500ml canning jar or lidded plastic container. Put the sliced vegetables on top of the soup base, followed by the noodles. Store in the fridge until needed.

3. When you're ready to eat, pour over 1½ cups / 350ml of boiling water, making sure everything is submerged. Place a lid on top and leave for 5 minutes. When ready, pour into a large bowl and enjoy!

Preparation time: *10 minutes*
Soaking time: *5 minutes*

Ingredients (Serves 1)

1 medium carrot, *top sliced off*
1 small pepper, *halved and seeded*
3 radishes
2 green onions
1 (1-inch / 2.5cm) piece of ginger, *finely grated*
1 tbsp miso
1 tbsp soy sauce
2 tbsp kimchi, *plus 1 tbsp brine*
¾ oz / 20g edamame noodles, *slightly crushed*

Top-ups

Spinach leaves
Extra green onion

Swaps

Any 7-oz / 200g mix of vegetables
Whole-wheat noodles for edamame noodles
Gochujang for miso

15–20g **8**
FIBER PLANTS

Kefir Curried Chickpeas

Preparation time: *5 minutes*
Cook time: *15 minutes*

Ingredients (Serves 2)

1 tsp cumin seeds
1 tsp yellow mustard seeds
2 (14-oz / 400g) cans chickpeas, *drained*
1 red pepper, *finely diced*
1 tbsp mild curry powder
2 tbsp Boosting Bouillon *(page 264)*
½ small Savoy cabbage, *cut into 1½-inch / 4cm wedges*
1 tbsp extra-virgin olive oil
8 curry leaves or 2 bay leaves
¼ cup / 60ml kefir
Zest and juice of ½ lemon
Salt and black pepper

Top-ups

Sauerkraut *(page 64)*
Tempeh Crumble *(page 266)*

Swap

Any beans for chickpeas

Kefir works in almost all recipes where you would use yogurt, packing in more bacterial strains for an extra probiotic boost. The diversity of plants and spices in this dish adds a variety of nutrients: chickpeas contain prebiotic fiber and dark, leafy-green Savoy cabbage contains more polyphenols than the lighter white variety.

Method

1. Place a large frying pan over medium heat and toast the cumin and mustard seeds for 30 seconds, until toasted and fragrant.

2. Add the chickpeas, red pepper, curry powder, Boosting Bouillon, and 2 cups / 500ml of hot water, then stir. Season with salt and pepper and bring to a boil, then reduce the heat and simmer. Cook for 10 minutes, until the liquid has almost completely reduced.

3. While the chickpeas are cooking, place a separate frying pan (one that has a lid) over high heat. Sear the cabbage wedges, without oil, for 2 minutes on each side, until charred. Add a splash of water to the pan, turn down the heat to medium, and then put the lid on, allowing the cabbage to steam for 5 minutes.

4. Heat the olive oil in a small frying pan until smoking and then add the curry leaves. Sizzle for 30 seconds, until fragrant, then remove from the heat.

5. Take the chickpeas off the heat and stir in the kefir, lemon zest, and lemon juice, check the seasoning, and then divide between two bowls. Top with the cabbage wedges and dress with the fried curry leaves and their oil.

Seeded Bruschetta Three Ways

These three seeded bruschetta variations are each unique in their own right, while sharing a fermented yogurt, miso, and tahini dressing, making it easy to make a couple, or all three, when friends are around to share. If you're savoring one of these recipes by yourself, you may end up with delicious leftovers for an extra snack or lunch tomorrow. Toasting the seeded bread gives extra crunch.

Harissa Mushrooms

5–10g FIBER **11** PLANTS

The combination of harissa and mushroom creates a great depth of flavor here. This recipe uses a portobello mushroom, but feel free to mix and match using whatever mushrooms you have on hand.

Preparation time: *5 minutes*
Cook time: *5 minutes*

Ingredients (Serves 1)

½ tbsp extra-virgin olive oil
1 large portobello mushroom or a handful of button mushrooms, *thinly sliced*
1 tsp harissa
1 tbsp Greek yogurt
½ tsp miso
1 tsp tahini
2 slices Nut-and-Seed Loaf (page 73), *toasted*
Salt and black pepper

Top-up

Sauerkraut (page 64)

Swap

Plant-based yogurt

Method

1. Heat the olive oil in a small frying pan, add the mushroom, and fry over high heat for 3–4 minutes. Add the harissa, season with salt and pepper, and set aside.

2. Mix the yogurt, miso, and tahini in a bowl and spread the mix onto the toasted bread. Top with the mushroom and serve.

Tricolore

5–10g FIBER **12** PLANTS

With the good fats from the avocado and the protein from the yogurt, this bruschetta will taste delicious and leave you satisfied. The tang of the balsamic vinegar and the fresh basil will create a symphony of flavors with each bite.

Preparation time: *5 minutes*

Ingredients (Serves 1)

4 cherry tomatoes, *quartered*
½ avocado, *coarsely chopped*
1 sprig of basil, *leaves picked and chopped*
1 tsp balsamic vinegar
1 tbsp Greek yogurt
½ tsp miso
1 tsp tahini
2 slices Nut-and-Seed Loaf *(page 73), toasted*
Salt and black pepper

Top-up

Sauerkraut *(page 64)*

Swap

Plant-based yogurt

Method

1. Mix the tomatoes, avocado, basil, and vinegar together in a bowl and season with salt and pepper.

2. In a separate bowl, mix the yogurt, miso, and tahini. Spread onto the toasted bread and top with the tomato mixture.

10–15g
FIBER

12
PLANTS

Kimchi Broccolini

Preparation time: *5 minutes*
Cook time: *10 minutes*

Ingredients (Serves 1)

2 stalks broccolini,
    halved lengthwise
1 tbsp extra-virgin olive oil
1 tbsp Greek yogurt
½ tsp miso
1 tsp tahini
2 slices Nut-and-Seed Loaf
    (page 73), toasted
2 tbsp kimchi
Salt and black pepper

Top-up

Seed Mix Sprinkle *(page 263)*

Swap

Plant-based yogurt

With three different ferments in one simple recipe, you'll have a delicious meal full of probiotic benefits in less than 15 minutes. It will leave you feeling wonderfully full and your gut microbes happy.

Method

1. Preheat the oven to 400°F / 200°C. Place the broccolini on a small baking sheet lined with parchment paper, toss with the olive oil and a pinch of salt and pepper, and roast for 8–10 minutes, until slightly charred.

2. Mix the Greek yogurt, miso, and tahini together. Spread onto the toasted bread and top with the cooked broccolini and kimchi.

Vibrant Salads

- 126 Lima Bean Caesar
- 129 Pomegranate-Lentil Salad
- 130 Roasted Broccolini–Tahini Salad
- 132 Eggplant Noodle Salad
- 134 Greens and Beans Salad
- 136 Red Pepper–Quinoa Salad
- 138 Pomegranate Tabbouleh
- 141 Polyphenol Salad
- 142 Carrot and Fennel Salad with Halloumi
- 145 Prebiotic Greek Salad
- 146 Bulgur Bowl
- 149 Kale and Mushroom Salad

Research shows that people who eat 30 different plants a week tend to have a more diverse gut microbiome than those who eat 10. This is why I aim for this target each week: a flourishing microbiome can help the body fight infections, reduce the risk of autoimmune disease, and regulate appetite and body weight, among other benefits.

Salads create a natural opportunity to easily achieve your 30 plants a week, and these ones are full of life, with hot and cold foods, satisfying textures, and every color of the rainbow. Consider each recipe as a framework rather than a rule, and substitute the ingredients with what's in season, available to you, and/or in your fridge. For dressings, a good-quality extra-virgin olive oil and vinegar will often do the trick, but the dressings in the Score Boosters chapter are also great here. Embrace all other manner of top-ups, like precooked grains or seed sprinkles. I hope you'll emerge from this chapter convinced, as I am, that salads aren't just for summer.

Lima Bean Caesar

15–20g FIBER **8** PLANTS

Crispy lima beans in place of croutons make this twist on a classic salad even better. We've also ramped up the plant count with cashews in the dressing, and you get added prebiotic fiber from the inulin in the artichokes—a feast for you and your gut microbes!

Method

1. Preheat the oven to 425°F / 220°C and line a baking sheet with parchment paper.

2. Put the dressing ingredients into a blender with 3 tablespoons of water and a pinch of salt and pepper and blend until smooth.

3. Put the lima beans onto the lined sheet, toss with the olive oil, season with salt and pepper, and spread out in a single layer. Roast for 15 minutes.

4. Place the lettuce, arugula, and artichokes in a large bowl with a pinch of salt and pepper, and toss with half the dressing. Divide between two plates and top with the lima beans. Drizzle with a little extra dressing to taste, or store any leftover dressing in the fridge for up to 1 week.

Preparation time: *15 minutes*
Cook time: *15 minutes*

Ingredients (Serves 2)

For the dressing

¼ cup / 35g cashews
1 tbsp capers plus 2 tbsp brine
1 garlic clove
2 tsp Dijon mustard
1 tbsp nutritional yeast
Zest and juice of ½ lemon
2 tbsp extra-virgin olive oil

1 (14-oz / 400g) can lima beans, drained
1 tbsp extra-virgin olive oil
1 head little gem lettuce, leaves separated
1 cup / 20g arugula
1 (10-oz / 285g) jar artichokes, drained (5¾ oz / 160g drained weight) and coarsely chopped
Salt and black pepper

Top-ups

Seed Mix Sprinkle (*page 263*)
Sauerkraut (*page 64*)
Anchovies

Swap

Any white beans for lima beans

VIBRANT SALADS

5–10g **6**
FIBER   PLANTS

Pomegranate-Lentil Salad

Preparation time: *20 minutes*

Ingredients (Serves 2)

1 avocado
Juice of 1 lime
¾ cup / 150g cooked black or green lentils
4½ oz / 130g cherry tomatoes, *quartered*
½ cup / 80g pomegranate seeds
Small handful of mint leaves, *coarsely chopped*
½ recipe Miso Dressing (page 270)
⅓ cup / 50g pumpkin seeds
Salt and black pepper

Top-ups

Sumac
Sauerkraut *(page 64)*
Seed Mix Sprinkle *(page 263)*

Swaps

Kimchi Dressing *(page 270)* for Miso Dressing
Pistachios for pumpkin seeds

The pleasant crunch of the pomegranate seeds and pumpkin seeds in this salad is a great contrast to the avocado and lentils, which are packed with fiber. Precooked packages are a great way to save time, but you can also batch-cook the lentils and store them in the fridge for a few days, or freeze for up to 1 month.

Method

1. Peel and dice the avocado and place in a large bowl with the lime juice. Toss to coat, then add the lentils, tomatoes, pomegranate seeds, and mint leaves to the bowl.

2. Pour over the dressing and toss once more to combine. Season with salt and pepper and serve topped with the pumpkin seeds.

Roasted Broccolini–Tahini Salad

10–15g FIBER **7** PLANTS

Along with adding protein, the tahini yogurt makes a delicious base for any roasted vegetables. You can also use a kefir-yogurt mix for added probiotic strains, and I enjoy using the sauce as a dip for raw veggies.

Method

1. Preheat the oven to 400°F / 200°C. Place the broccolini, chickpeas, and garlic on a large baking sheet lined with parchment paper, toss with 1 tablespoon of the olive oil and a pinch of salt and pepper, and roast for 20 minutes, until the broccolini is slightly charred and the chickpeas are turning crisp.

2. Mix the shallot, parsley, tomatoes, apple cider vinegar, and the remaining 4 tablespoons of olive oil together and season with salt and pepper.

3. Put the yogurt and tahini into a bowl and, when ready, squeeze the roasted garlic from its skin into the bowl. Mix to combine, adding 1–2 tablespoons of cold water if needed to thin. Spread the tahini yogurt onto two plates, then top with the broccolini, chickpeas, and tomatoes.

Preparation time: *10 minutes*
Cook time: *20 minutes*

Ingredients (Serves 2)

10 oz / 300g broccolini
1 (14-oz / 400g) can chickpeas, *drained and patted dry*
2 garlic cloves, *unpeeled*
5 tbsp extra-virgin olive oil
1 shallot, *finely chopped*
¾ cup / 30g finely chopped parsley
¾ cup / 130g cherry tomatoes, *halved*
2 tbsp apple cider vinegar
⅓ cup plus 1 tbsp / 90g Greek yogurt
2 tbsp tahini
Salt and black pepper

Top-ups

Seed Mix Sprinkle (*page 263*)
Sauerkraut (*page 64*)
Nut Crumb (*page 262*)

Swaps

Any white beans for chickpeas
Cashew Cream (*page 268*) for yogurt
Any fresh herb for parsley

Eggplant Noodle Salad

10–15g FIBER **5** PLANTS

I love eggplant, and this is a great way to use whatever vegetables you have in the fridge to accompany it. If you can find them, soybean (edamame) noodles are packed with fiber and protein and make a great alternative to whole-wheat egg noodles. No need to buy special smoked tofu here—make your own by sprinkling smoked paprika over regular tofu.

Method

1. Preheat the oven to 425°F / 220°C and line a baking sheet with parchment paper. In a large bowl, cover the noodles with boiling water and set aside.

2. Lay the eggplant on the lined baking sheet, drizzle with the olive oil, season with salt and pepper, and roast in the oven for 20–25 minutes, until soft and slightly charred.

3. Put the miso dressing, cilantro, and spinach into a blender and blend until smooth. Add a tablespoon of water to thin if necessary.

4. Drain the noodles and add to a bowl with the sliced veggies, tofu, and three-quarters of the dressing. Toss to combine and serve topped with the eggplant, with the remaining dressing drizzled on top.

Preparation time: *20 minutes*
Cook time: *20 minutes*

Ingredients (Serves 2)

3½ oz / 100g whole-wheat egg noodles
1 eggplant, *cut into ¾-inch / 2cm chunks*
2 tbsp extra-virgin olive oil
10 oz / 300g mixed vegetables of choice, *thinly sliced*
3½ oz / 100g smoked tofu, *cubed*
Salt and black pepper

For the dressing

1 recipe Miso Dressing (*page 270*)
Handful of cilantro
Handful of fresh spinach

Top-ups

Seed Mix Sprinkle (*page 263*)
Tempeh Crumble (*page 266*)
Fresh chile

Swaps

Plain tofu for smoked tofu
Soybean (edamame) noodles for whole-wheat egg noodles

VIBRANT SALADS

Greens and Beans Salad

10–15g **8**
FIBER PLANTS

VIBRANT SALADS

With its grapefruit segments, this salad is a real showstopper. The black beans bring polyphenols to the plate, and the frozen peas pack in vitamin C, plant protein, and fiber. Toast the pumpkin seeds in a dry frying pan for the most delicious taste and texture.

Method

1. Spread the dressing out onto a flat serving plate. Arrange the arugula, peas, black beans, avocado, and grapefruit slices on top.

2. Scatter the pumpkin seeds and pickled green chiles (if using) all over, season with salt and pepper, and serve immediately.

Preparation time: *20 minutes*

Ingredients (Serves 2)

½ recipe Kefir Dressing
 (page 271)
2 cups / 40g arugula
½ cup / 65g frozen peas, *defrosted*
1 (14-oz / 400g) can black beans, *drained*
1 avocado, *sliced and dressed with 1 tbsp lemon juice*
1 grapefruit, *peeled and sliced into segments*
¼ cup / 30g pumpkin seeds
3 pickled green chiles, *chopped (optional)*
Salt and black pepper

Top-ups

Nut Crumb *(page 262)*
Tempeh Crumble *(page 266)*

Swap

Green lentils for black beans

Red Pepper–Quinoa Salad

10–15g **7**
FIBER PLANTS

This recipe is economical in its use of ingredients, as two of the three elements you need for the dressing also appear in the salad. The peppers have more vitamin C than an orange, and the protein and fiber content of quinoa is far superior to that of rice. Choose any color of quinoa that you fancy—or a mix, to boost your plant count.

Method

Put all of the ingredients in a bowl with the dressing and toss to coat. Season to taste with salt and pepper.

Preparation time: *15 minutes*

Ingredients (Serves 2)

⅔ cup / 120g cooked quinoa
1¼ cups / 160g frozen peas, *defrosted*
½ cup / 70g olives, *halved*
2 roasted red peppers from a jar, *thinly sliced*
½ cup / 60g chopped hazelnuts
2 tbsp Sauerkraut *(page 64)*
½ recipe Sauerkraut Dressing *(page 271)*
Salt and black pepper

Top-ups

Mixed ACV Pickles *(page 269)*
Tempeh Crumble *(page 266)*
Feta
Fresh or frozen herbs

Swap

Kimchi Dressing *(page 270)* for Sauerkraut Dressing

VIBRANT SALADS

Pomegranate Tabbouleh

5–10g FIBER   **11** PLANTS

The abundance of herbs in this refreshing recipe all count toward your 30 plants a week, and the pomegranate seeds bring delicious pops of sweetness to the fresh, zingy mix. Tabbouleh lasts really well in the fridge, and the flavors get even better the next day, so this is a great dish to prepare in advance of a busy week.

Method

1. Place the bulgur in a bowl and cover with ⅔ cup / 160ml boiling water. Cover and allow to soak for 20 minutes, until the liquid has been absorbed.

2. Finely chop the herbs and add to a bowl along with the vegetables, pomegranate seeds, and bulgur.

3. Mix the lemon juice, olive oil, garlic, and pickled chiles together with a pinch of salt and pepper, add to the bowl, and toss to combine.

Preparation time: *20 minutes*

Ingredients (Serves 4)

- ⅔ cup / 100g bulgur
- 2½ cups / 50g tightly packed parsley
- 3 cups / 30g dill sprigs
- 2½ cups / 30g lightly packed mint leaves
- 7 tbsp / 20g chives
- 10 oz / 260g cherry tomatoes, *quartered*
- 1 cucumber, *finely diced*
- 6 green onions, *thinly sliced*
- 1⅓ cups / 200g pomegranate seeds
- Juice of 2 lemons
- 6 tbsp extra-virgin olive oil
- 2 garlic cloves, *finely grated*
- 6 pickled green chiles, *finely chopped*
- Salt and black pepper

Top-ups

Tempeh Crumble (*page 266*)
Sauerkraut (*page 64*)

Swap

Quinoa for bulgur

VIBRANT SALADS

10–15g **5**
FIBER   PLANTS

Polyphenol Salad

Preparation time: *20 minutes*
Cook time: *30 minutes*

Ingredients *(Serves 2)*

3 purple/orange carrots, *peeled, halved, and cut into 1-inch / 2.5cm pieces*
½ red cabbage, *core removed and sliced into thin wedges*
½ cauliflower, *cut into large chunks, stalk included*
3 tbsp extra-virgin olive oil
½ head radicchio
½ recipe Kimchi Dressing *(page 270)*
2 tbsp pumpkin seeds
Salt and black pepper

Top-ups

Extra kimchi
Savory Crispy Pulses and Grains *(page 267)*
Can of white beans

Swaps

Any lettuce for radicchio
Any root vegetables

The rainbow color of this salad indicates that it's packed full of polyphenols. Choosing darker or purple varieties of carrots and cauliflower will increase the polyphenol count, but the standard versions are also nutritious. Plus, the radicchio and red cabbage do a lot of heavy lifting for you polyphenol-wise. Soaking the radicchio in ice water for 30 minutes will reduce its bitterness.

Method

1. Preheat the oven to 400°F / 200°C and line a baking sheet with parchment paper. Lay the carrots, cabbage, and cauliflower on the sheet, drizzle the olive oil all over, season with salt and pepper, and roast in the oven for 30 minutes, tossing halfway through.

2. When ready, allow to cool slightly and transfer to a large bowl with the radicchio, Kimchi Dressing, and pumpkin seeds. Toss to coat, season one last time, and serve.

Carrot and Fennel Salad with Halloumi

5–10g FIBER   **7** PLANTS

The blush colors of the carrot and fennel dressed in kefir make this a stunning centerpiece as well as a satisfying salad. Sumac and orange bring out a lovely citrus flavor; when they're in season, my favorite blood oranges would be especially good here. Feel free to use tofu instead of halloumi as a vegan alternative.

Method

1. Using the slicer attachment in a food processor, thinly slice the carrots and fennel. You can also use a mandoline if you prefer.

2. Put the orange zest and juice, tahini, kefir, and sumac in a large bowl and mix together until smooth. Thin with 1–2 tablespoons of cold water if necessary and season with salt and pepper. Add the sliced vegetables and cilantro to the dressing and toss until coated.

3. Turn your broiler to its highest setting and lay the halloumi on a nonstick baking sheet, drizzle the olive oil all over, and place under the broiler for 3–4 minutes on each side, until golden.

4. Divide the salad between two plates and place the grilled halloumi on top. Scatter the pistachios all over, along with the reserved fennel fronds, and serve.

Preparation time: *15 minutes*
Cook time: *8 minutes*

Ingredients (Serves 2)

2 carrots, peeled
1 fennel bulb, stalks removed and fronds reserved
Zest of ½ orange plus 2 tbsp juice
2 tbsp tahini
6 tbsp / 90ml kefir
1 tbsp sumac
½ cup / 20g cilantro, coarsely chopped
5¼ oz / 150g halloumi, cut into 6 slices
1 tsp extra-virgin olive oil
¼ cup / 25g coarsely chopped pistachios
Salt and black pepper

Top-ups

Nut Crumb (page 262)
Tempeh Crumble (page 266)
Sumac

Swap

Cashew Cream (page 268) for kefir
Tofu for halloumi

VIBRANT SALADS

5–10g
FIBER

6
PLANTS

Prebiotic Greek Salad

Preparation time: *15 minutes*

Ingredients *(Serves 2)*

1⅓ cups / 220g cherry tomatoes, *halved*
1 cucumber, *cut into 1-inch / 2.5cm chunks*
1 (10-oz / 285g) jar artichokes, *drained and coarsely chopped (5¾ oz / 160g drained weight)*
⅓ cup / 50g pitted olives
2 tbsp extra-virgin olive oil
1 tbsp apple cider vinegar
3 cups / 60g arugula
¼ cup / 35g chopped hazelnuts
2 oz / 60g feta cheese, *crumbled*
Salt and black pepper

Top-ups

Seed Mix Sprinkle *(page 263)*
Tempeh Crumble *(page 266)*

Swap

Pumpkin or sunflower seeds for hazelnuts

I'm transported to the Mediterranean with this salad, no matter the weather. If you're preparing it in advance, wait to toss the vegetables and dressing with the arugula until just before serving, as the acid from the apple cider vinegar will spoil the arugula. Polyphenol-rich olives and prebiotic-packed artichokes will help you feel your best.

Method

1. Put the tomatoes, cucumber, artichokes, and olives into a bowl with the olive oil and apple cider vinegar. Season with salt and pepper and toss to combine.

2. Just before serving, toss together with the arugula. Finish with the hazelnuts and feta cheese.

Bulgur Bowl

5–10g FIBER **10** PLANTS

Double the quantities of roasted vegetables in this recipe and you'll set yourself up with a great base for other meals. We mix up our grains and use bulgur wheat here instead of couscous or rice for diversity. Using different-colored peppers will add another tick toward your 30 plants a week. Roasting the vegetables in an air fryer, if you have one, will make preparation even easier.

Method

1. Preheat the oven to 400°F / 200°C and line a large baking sheet with parchment paper.

2. Lay the prepared vegetables on the lined sheet, drizzle the olive oil all over, season with salt and pepper, toss to coat, and roast in the oven for 25–35 minutes, stirring halfway through, until soft and slightly charred.

3. Place the bulgur in a bowl with a pinch of salt and cover with ⅓ cup / 80ml boiling water. Cover and leave to soak for 20 minutes, until the grains have puffed up and absorbed the liquid.

4. Toss the roasted vegetables, bulgur, basil, and dressing together until combined. Scatter the seed mix on top and serve.

Preparation time: *15 minutes*
Cook time: *25 minutes*

Ingredients (Serves 2)

1 eggplant, *cut into ⅜-inch / 1cm cubes*
1 zucchini, *cut into ⅜-inch / 1cm cubes*
1 red onion, *coarsely chopped*
2 bell peppers, *cut into 3/8-inch / 1cm cubes*
3 tbsp extra-virgin olive oil
⅓ cup / 50g bulgur
¾ cup / 15g tightly packed basil leaves, *roughly torn*
½ recipe Sauerkraut Dressing *(page 271)*
2 tbsp Seed Mix Sprinkle *(page 263)*
Salt and black pepper

Top-ups

Nut Crumb *(page 262)*
Tempeh Crumble *(page 266)*

Swaps

Kimchi Dressing *(page 270)* for Sauerkraut Dressing
Pearl barley for bulgur *(allow longer cooking time)*

VIBRANT SALADS

15–20g
FIBER

9
PLANTS

Kale and Mushroom Salad

Preparation time: *15 minutes*
Cook time: *20 minutes*

Ingredients (Serves 2)

1 (14-oz / 400g) can beans, *drained and patted dry*
10 oz / 300g cremini mushrooms, *thinly sliced*
2 tbsp extra-virgin olive oil
5 tbsp tahini
4 pickled green chiles, *sliced, plus 3 tbsp of their brine*
6 oz / 170g kale, *shredded*
2 tbsp Sauerkraut *(page 64)*
3 tbsp Seed Mix Sprinkle *(page 263)*
Salt and black pepper

Top-up

Tempeh Crumble *(page 266)*

Swap

Chickpeas for beans

Take tips from this recipe and use them in your cooking elsewhere. For example, don't throw away the brine from your pickled foods—it's a great way to add flavor to dressings, like in this salad. Massage your kale to soften it if you're eating it raw, and if you use a mix of kale and lacinato kale, you'll be earning extra plant points. In this recipe, you can use whatever beans you like.

Method

1. Preheat the oven to 400°F / 200°C and line a large baking sheet with parchment paper. Spread out the beans and mushrooms on the baking sheet, toss with the olive oil, season with salt and pepper, then roast in the oven for 20 minutes, until the mushrooms are soft and the beans are starting to crisp at the edges.

2. Put the tahini and pickling brine from the chiles into a large bowl and mix until smooth. Add a few tablespoons of cold water if necessary to get the consistency of heavy cream. Season with salt and pepper.

3. Add the kale to the bowl and use your hands to massage the dressing into the kale until it has softened slightly and is thoroughly coated.

4. When the mushrooms and beans are ready, add them to the kale along with the sliced pickled chiles and sauerkraut. Toss and serve topped with the seed mix.

Satisfying Mains

- 152 Eggplant Parmigiana
- 154 Cashew-Cream Green Curry
- 157 Mushroom Stroganoff with Lima Bean Mash
- 158 Diversity Dal
- 160 Sheet-Pan Artichoke and Olive Bake
- 163 11-Plant Orzo
- 164 Eggplant Schnitzel
- 166 Asparagus–Pearl Barley Risotto
- 169 Palak Tofu
- 171 Zucchini Lima Beans with Tomato Salsa
- 172 Sheet-Pan Harissa Cabbage
- 174 Broccolini and Walnut Orecchiette

Never underestimate the importance of *enjoying* your food. Certain dishes can evoke happy memories or bring comfort, such as a filling pasta on a rainy day or a spicy curry on a Friday night. The love we feel for these comforting dishes is to be cherished, and they are uniquely capable of making us feel our best.

I grew up on a diet of meat and two vegetables, but through my research I've learned that this way of eating can be improved. When we put the focus on meat, we don't leave space on our plate for the plant diversity and fiber that our gut bacteria need. In this chapter, we've created delicious meals that give you that wonderful feeling of satisfaction while also nourishing your gut. With pleasure in mind, we've included dishes like a twist on my favorite schnitzel from my time in Austria, which will always evoke happy memories for me. A lot of these recipes can be batch-cooked, making them perfect for quick weeknight meals that recharge you from the inside out.

Eggplant Parmigiana

10–15g FIBER   **7** PLANTS

What could be more comforting than an eggplant parmigiana? We've given this classic a gut-health twist by adding fiber-packed lentils, but this will work just as well with any bean. Add a mix of both lentils and beans to increase the fiber and plant protein in this dish, making it even more hearty and satisfying.

Method

1. Preheat the oven to 400°F / 200°C. Line a large baking sheet with parchment paper and lay out the eggplant slices in a single layer. Season with salt and pepper and drizzle 1 tablespoon of the olive oil all over. Bake for 25 minutes, until golden and soft.

2. Meanwhile, place a frying pan over medium heat and sauté the onion in the remaining tablespoon of olive oil for 3 minutes, until softened. Add the garlic and chile and cook for 1 minute more. Pour in the tomatoes and lentils, then half fill the tomato can with water and add this to the pan too. Simmer for 10 minutes, until slightly thickened. Add the basil and cook for 5 minutes more, then season with salt and pepper.

3. Spoon a third of the mixture into the base of an 8- or 9-inch / 20–23cm square ovenproof dish (or similar) and top with a layer of eggplant. Repeat this twice more, then finish with the mozzarella and Parmesan.

4. Bake for 30 minutes, until the cheese is bubbling and golden brown. Serve with some steamed greens.

Preparation time: *15 minutes*
Cook time: *1 hour*

Ingredients *(Serves 4 with leftovers)*

3 eggplants, *sliced lengthwise into ⅜-inch / 1cm-thick slices*
2 tbsp extra-virgin olive oil
1 onion, *finely chopped*
2 garlic cloves, *coarsely chopped*
1 small fresh red chile, *thinly sliced*
1 (14-oz / 400g) can diced tomatoes
1 (14-oz / 400g) can black or green lentils, *drained*
1½ cups / 30g basil, *leaves torn, plus a few to garnish*
1 (4½-oz / 125g) ball of mozzarella, *torn*
⅔ cup / 20g finely grated Parmesan cheese
Salt and black pepper

Top-ups

Kimchi
Extra basil

Swaps

Black-eyed peas for lentils
Vegan cheese

SATISFYING MAINS

Cashew-Cream Green Curry

10–15g FIBER   **11** PLANTS

The plant count in this dish will send you well on your way to your weekly 30. A top tip is to make more curry paste than you need and store the remainder in the freezer for a quick meal another day. I love the flexibility of this dish; the sauce is a great base for adding any vegetables and proteins of your choice, such as tofu, shrimp, or chicken. Serve this with Pearls and Puy (page 265) or rice.

Method

1. First, make the curry paste. Put the cilantro, onion, garlic, chile, ginger, lemongrass, and lime zest into the bowl of a food processor and blend until finely chopped. You may need to scrape down the sides of the bowl a couple of times.

2. Heat the olive oil in a large saucepan and fry the curry paste for 3–4 minutes, stirring all the time. Add the coconut milk, the black beans and their liquid, and ¾ cup plus 2 tablespoons / 200ml of water and simmer for 5 minutes to allow the flavors to infuse.

3. Stir in the Cashew Cream and vegetables. Mix well and simmer for 5–7 minutes, until the vegetables are tender but still a little crunchy.

4. Finish the curry with the fish sauce and squeeze over the reserved limes. Season to taste with salt and pepper.

Preparation time: *15 minutes*
Cook time: *15 minutes*

Ingredients (Serves 4)

For the curry paste

3½ oz / 100g cilantro
1 onion, *quartered*
2 garlic cloves
1 small fresh green chile
1¾ oz / 50g fresh ginger, *coarsely chopped*
1 lemongrass stalk, *smashed and tough outer leaves removed*
Zest of 2 limes *(reserve the zested limes for squeezing)*

3 tbsp extra-virgin olive oil
1 (14-fl oz / 400ml) can coconut milk
1 (14-oz / 400g) can black beans and their liquid
1 recipe Cashew Cream *(page 268)*
1 head broccoli, *cut into florets*
7 oz / 200g green beans, *coarsely chopped*
6 oz / 180g snow peas
1 tbsp fish sauce
Salt and black pepper

Top-up

Kimchi

Swaps

Coconut milk for Cashew Cream
Soy sauce for fish sauce

Mushroom Stroganoff with Lima Bean Mash

10–15g **7**
FIBER PLANTS

Preparation time: *15 minutes*
Cook time: *20 minutes*

Ingredients (Serves 4)

2 (14-oz / 400g) cans lima beans, *drained (reserve some liquid)*
2 tbsp extra-virgin olive oil
1 onion, *thinly sliced*
3 garlic cloves, *coarsely chopped*
1½ lb / 700g mushrooms, *sliced*
1½ tbsp Dijon mustard
1 tsp paprika
1¼ cups / 180g cooked chestnuts, *coarsely chopped*
7 oz / 200g baby spinach
⅓ cup / 85ml kefir
Salt and black pepper

Top-ups

Sauerkraut (*page 64*)
Harissa
Tempeh Crumble (*page 266*)

Swap

6 tbsp / 100ml Cashew Cream (*page 268*) **for kefir**

Mushrooms are a favorite of mine, not only for their health benefits but also for their culinary versatility and flavor. Choose whichever variety you like best for this dish or—even better—a mix. The lima beans are a great alternative to mashed potatoes, with loads more fiber, and you'll receive fantastic gut-health benefits from the probiotics in the kefir. Just be sure to stir it through at the very end.

Method

1. Add the lima beans to a food processor with a pinch of salt and pepper. Blend until almost smooth, adding a little liquid from the can if the mash is too thick. Transfer to a medium saucepan.

2. To make the stroganoff, heat the olive oil in a large lidded frying pan and sauté the onion for 3 minutes over medium heat, until translucent. Add the garlic and cook for 30 seconds more, then add the mushrooms to the pan and mix together. Cover and cook for 7 minutes, stirring occasionally, until the mushrooms are soft and turning golden.

3. Add the mustard, paprika, and chestnuts and cook for 1 minute. Turn off the heat and add the spinach, stirring to combine, then place the lid on top and leave to rest for 5 minutes, to allow the spinach to wilt.

4. Place the lima bean mash over medium heat and stir until heated through.

5. Remove the lid from the stroganoff, add the kefir, and stir everything together until combined. Season to taste and serve with the mash.

Diversity Dal

15–20g FIBER **14** PLANTS

SATISFYING MAINS

The colors and plant diversity of this dish signal the true cornucopia of polyphenols here. The yellow split peas add a satisfying texture, and the spices and herbs bring the plant score of this dish up to a new level. You can use fresh or frozen spinach, and swap miso for the Boosting Bouillon, if you prefer.

Method

1. Heat the olive oil in a saucepan over medium heat and sauté the onion for 5 minutes, until softened. Add the garlic, ginger, and chile and cook for 1 minute more, then stir in the spices and mix to combine.

2. Add the lentils, yellow split peas, quinoa, Boosting Bouillon (if using), and 5 cups / 1.2L of water, bring to a boil, and then reduce to a gentle simmer. Cover and cook for 15 minutes.

3. Add the butternut squash and cook for another 30 minutes, until the squash is soft—add a splash of water if the dal starts to dry out. Stir in the spinach 5 minutes before the end of the cooking time, allowing 1–2 minutes longer if using frozen spinach. Season to taste with salt and pepper before serving. The dal may thicken when it is cooled, so add a splash of water to thin if necessary when reheating.

Preparation time: 20 minutes
Cook time: 50 minutes

Ingredients (Serves 4)

2 tbsp extra-virgin olive oil
1 onion, *finely chopped*
2 garlic cloves, *finely chopped*
1 (1-inch / 2.5cm) piece of ginger, *finely grated*
1 small fresh red chile, *finely chopped*
2 tbsp curry powder
1 tbsp cumin seeds
1 tsp garam masala
½ cup / 100g split red lentils
½ cup / 100g yellow split peas
½ cup / 100g quinoa
2 tbsp Boosting Bouillon (optional; page 264)
½ butternut squash, *peeled and cut into ¾-inch / 2cm cubes*
4 oz / 120g frozen or fresh spinach
Salt and black pepper

Top-ups

Seed Mix Sprinkle (page 263)
Soft-boiled egg
Kefir

Swaps

Miso for Boosting Bouillon
Any vegetable for squash

Sheet-Pan Artichoke and Olive Bake

15–20g FIBER   **5** PLANTS

Most of the ingredients in this satisfying sheet-pan bake start off in your pantry, but if you're making this out of zucchini season, it will work with other vegetables, like leeks. Add extras of your choice to increase the plant score. The olives are packed with polyphenols, while the jarred artichokes are bursting with prebiotics.

Method

1. Preheat the oven to 400°F / 200°C and line a large baking sheet with parchment paper. Spread the artichokes, cranberry beans, and olives onto the sheet, toss with 2 tablespoons of the olive oil, and season with a pinch of salt and pepper.

2. Lay the zucchini on top, drizzle with the remaining olive oil, and season with salt and pepper. Roast in the oven for 15 minutes.

3. Carefully remove from the oven, scatter the feta cheese all over the zucchini, and return to the oven for a further 15 minutes, until the feta has melted and the zucchini and artichokes are browning at the edges. Scatter with the chopped parsley and serve with wedges of lemon for squeezing over.

Preparation time: *5 minutes*
Cook time: *30 minutes*

Ingredients (Serves 4)

1 (10-oz / 285g) jar artichokes, *drained and coarsely chopped (5¾ oz / 160g drained weight)*
2 (14-oz / 400g) cans cranberry beans, *drained*
⅔ cup / 100g pitted olives
3 tbsp extra-virgin olive oil
3 zucchini, *quartered lengthwise*
2½ oz / 70g feta
Small handful of parsley, *coarsely chopped*
1 lemon, *quartered*
Salt and black pepper

Top-ups

Kimchi
Sauerkraut Dressing
   (page 271)
Savory Crispy Pulses and Grains
   (page 267)

Swaps

Broccoli for zucchini
Mozzarella for feta, or skip the cheese

SATISFYING MAINS

5–10g
FIBER

11
PLANTS

11-Plant Orzo

Preparation time: *15 minutes*
Cook time: *35 minutes*

Ingredients (Serves 4)

2 tbsp extra-virgin olive oil
1 onion, *finely chopped*
3 garlic cloves, *coarsely chopped*
2 bell peppers, *different colors, seeded and thinly sliced*
2 zucchini, *sliced into ¼-inch / ½cm-thick rounds*
1 leek, *halved and thinly sliced*
2 (14-oz / 400g) cans diced tomatoes
1 (14-oz / 400g) can navy beans and their liquid
⅔ cup / 120g orzo
⅔ cup / 100g pitted olives
1 tsp paprika
1 tbsp miso
2½ cups / 30g lightly packed fresh basil leaves, *torn, plus a few to garnish*
Juice of ½ lemon
Salt and black pepper

Top-ups

Sauerkraut (page 64)
Cod

Swaps

Any canned beans for navy beans
Nutritional yeast for miso

The inspiration for this dish comes from a Catalan dish I love called bacalao a la llauna, where cod is baked in the oven with a mountain of Mediterranean vegetables. Without the cod, it's full of fiber and plants, but feel free to add grilled or salt cod here if you prefer. Adding peppers of two different colors will improve the mix of polyphenols and plant diversity.

Method

1. Heat the olive oil in a large Dutch oven (12-inch / 30cm diameter or similar) over medium heat. Fry the onion for 3 minutes, until softened, then add the garlic and fry for 30 seconds more.

2. Stir in the peppers, zucchini, and leek, cover, reduce the heat, and gently cook for 5–8 minutes, until just softened. Add the tomatoes, navy beans and their liquid, the orzo, olives, paprika, miso, basil, and a pinch of salt and pepper, and stir until the vegetables are thoroughly coated with the sauce and the orzo is evenly dispersed.

3. Bring to a boil, lower the heat, and simmer with the lid on for 10 minutes, then turn off the heat and allow to rest for 10 minutes to allow the orzo to fully cook and absorb the stock. (If you are serving with cod fillets, nestle these into the orzo 5 minutes before the end of the cooking time, then turn off the heat and leave to rest, being sure not to remove the lid.)

4. Squeeze the lemon juice all over before serving.

Eggplant Schnitzel

5–10g FIBER **10** PLANTS

This is a healthy spin on my favorite Wiener schnitzel from my younger days in Austria—I find the Nut Crumb a delicious and welcome departure from breadcrumbs. When frying the schnitzel, beware that the nuts can burn quickly and become bitter, so keep the heat at medium and your eye on the pan, and give them no more than a minute on each side.

Preparation time: *15 minutes*
Cook time: *25 minutes*

Ingredients (Serves 2)

1 large eggplant, *sliced lengthwise into 4*
1 tbsp harissa
2 tbsp extra-virgin olive oil, *plus extra to garnish*
1¾ oz / 50g Edam cheese, *coarsely grated*
1 medium egg, *beaten*
2¾ oz / 80g Nut Crumb *(page 262)*
⅓ cup / 80g hummus
2½ cups / 50g arugula
2 tbsp Sauerkraut *(page 64)*
Salt and black pepper

Top-up

Kimchi Dressing *(page 270)*

Swaps

2 tbsp extra-virgin olive oil for the egg
Cheddar cheese for Edam

Method

1. Preheat the oven to 400°F / 200°C, line a baking sheet with parchment paper, and lay the eggplant slices on the baking sheet.

2. Mix the harissa with 1 tablespoon of the olive oil, then brush this all over the eggplant slices on both sides. Season with salt and pepper and bake in the oven for 20 minutes, until tender and turning golden.

3. When ready, allow the eggplant to cool slightly. Spread the grated cheese all over the surface of two slices of eggplant. Place the remaining eggplant slices on top, pressing down firmly, creating two "sandwiches." Dip each one into the egg, and then into the Nut Crumb, pressing the crumb into each side of the eggplant to make sure it sticks and the eggplant is evenly coated.

4. Place a large frying pan over medium heat with the remaining tablespoon of olive oil. When hot, fry the eggplant schnitzel for 1 minute on each side, until the nuts are golden and crisp—you can fry for a little longer if necessary; just make sure the nuts do not burn.

5. Divide the hummus between two plates, top with the arugula and sauerkraut, and place the schnitzel on top.

Asparagus–Pearl Barley Risotto

5–10g FIBER   **6** PLANTS

Few dishes are more comforting than risotto, but with less than 0.5g of fiber per 3½ oz / 100g in risotto rice, I wanted to create a version that's better for my gut health and blood sugar. Pearl barley has over 10 times more fiber, helping me stay energized for longer. If asparagus is not in season, try another green vegetable, such as broccoli.

Method

1. Preheat the oven to 400°F / 200°C.

2. Heat the olive oil in a Dutch oven over medium heat and sauté the leek with a pinch of salt for 3 minutes, stirring occasionally. Add the garlic and cook for 1 minute more.

3. Add the pearl barley, lentils, and wine. Simmer for 1 minute and then add 2½ cups / 600ml of water and the Boosting Bouillon. Bring to a boil, place a tight-fitting lid on top, and transfer to the oven for 25 minutes.

4. Carefully remove the Dutch oven from the oven and stir in the asparagus and Parmesan. Replace the lid and return to the oven for 10 minutes.

5. Allow the risotto to cool slightly before stirring in the kefir, to keep the kefir from separating. Scatter over the parsley and season to taste with salt and pepper.

Preparation time: *10 minutes*
Cook time: *40 minutes*

Ingredients (Serves 3–4)

- **1 tbsp extra-virgin olive oil**
- **1 medium leek,** *trimmed and thinly sliced*
- **2 garlic cloves,** *coarsely chopped*
- **½ cup / 100g pearl barley**
- **⅓ cup / 70g green (Puy) lentils**
- **6½ tbsp / 100ml white wine**
- **2 tbsp Boosting Bouillon** (*page 264*)
- **14 oz / 400g asparagus,** *tough parts of the stalks discarded, finely chopped*
- **1¾ oz / 50g finely grated Parmesan cheese**
- **3 tbsp kefir**
- **⅓ cup / 15g finely chopped parsley**
- **Salt and black pepper**

Top-ups

Sauerkraut (*page 64*)
Nut Crumb (*page 262*)

Swaps

Nutritional yeast for Parmesan
Broccoli for asparagus
Miso for Boosting Bouillon

5–10g FIBER **12** PLANTS

Palak Tofu

Preparation time: *20 minutes*
Cook time: *30 minutes*

Ingredients (Serves 4)

12 oz / 350g firm tofu,
 cut into ¾-inch / 2cm cubes
3 tbsp extra-virgin olive oil
2 tsp garam masala
1 small fresh green chile,
 coarsely chopped
⅓ cup / 40g cashews
18 oz / 500g frozen spinach,
 defrosted
1 onion, *finely chopped*
2 plum tomatoes,
 coarsely chopped
3 garlic cloves, *finely grated*
1 (2½-inch / 5cm) piece of
 ginger, *finely grated*
2 tsp ground cumin
2 tsp ground coriander
Juice of ½ lemon
Pearls and Puy (*page 265*),
 to serve
Salt and black pepper

Top-ups

Sauerkraut (*page 64*)
Cilantro leaves
Fresh chile, chopped or sliced

Swap

Paneer or chickpeas for tofu

The deep, vibrant green of this dish is a sight to behold; the many spices add to your plant count and are great for your gut microbiome. Frozen spinach makes up the bulk of this iron-packed sauce—cooking with onions and garlic and adding lemon juice at the end will help your body absorb that iron. If tofu isn't your thing, try it with paneer or chickpeas instead.

Method

1. Preheat the oven to 400°F / 200°C. Line a large baking sheet with paper towels and lay the cubes of tofu on top in a single layer. Place more paper towels on top, then top with something heavy to press down firmly and extract the excess liquid from the tofu. Leave for 10 minutes.

2. Transfer the drained tofu to a bowl and toss with 1 tablespoon of the olive oil, 1 teaspoon of the garam masala, and some salt and pepper. Line the same baking sheet with parchment paper, lay the tofu on it in a single layer, and bake in the oven for 20 minutes.

3. Heat another tablespoon of olive oil in a large frying pan and add the chile, half the cashews, and the spinach, along with any excess liquid from its being defrosted. Add ⅔ cup / 150ml of water and simmer for 5 minutes. Allow to cool slightly, then transfer to a blender or food processor and blend until smooth.

4. Return the pan to the heat with the remaining tablespoon of olive oil and sauté the onion and tomatoes for 5 minutes, until soft and caramelized. Add the garlic, ginger, cumin, coriander, and the remaining teaspoon of garam masala and cook for 1 minute more. Pour the blended spinach back into the pan and heat through.

5. Stir in the baked tofu, remaining cashews, and lemon juice and season with salt and pepper before serving with the Pearls and Puy.

20–25g
FIBER

9
PLANTS

Zucchini Lima Beans with Tomato Salsa

Preparation time: *15 minutes*
Cook time: *20 minutes*

Ingredients (Serves 2 with leftovers)

4 tbsp extra-virgin olive oil
2 shallots, *finely chopped*
1 zucchini, *thinly sliced*
1 garlic clove, *finely chopped*
2 (14-oz / 400g) cans lima beans and their liquid
4 oz / 120g broccoli, *cut into small florets, coarsely chopped*
Zest of 1 lemon
1 small fresh red chile, *thinly sliced*
2 tbsp Seed Mix Sprinkle (page 263)
Salt and black pepper

For the salsa

15 cherry tomatoes, *quartered*
Small handful each of dill, parsley, and basil
1½ tbsp capers
Juice of ½ lemon

Top-ups

Kimchi
Nut Crumb (page 262)
Toasted sourdough

Swap

Any white beans for lima beans

Your gut microbes will be satisfied with their favorite Ingredient, beans, and cooking them with zucchini means this creamy dish has added fiber. The vibrant tomato salsa adds a burst of freshness here, while the seed mix incorporates a delicious crunch and added plant points. This is a perfect midweek main, as it's so quick and easy to make.

Method

1. Heat 1 tablespoon of the olive oil in a large frying pan and sauté the shallots over medium heat for 1 minute, until slightly softened. Add the zucchini slices and cook for 8 minutes, until softened and caramelized, stirring occasionally. Stir in the garlic and cook for 1 minute more.

2. Add the lima beans with their liquid, the broccoli, and the lemon zest. Stir and season with salt and pepper, then reduce the heat and simmer for 6–7 minutes, until the sauce has thickened and the broccoli is tender but retains a bit of bite.

3. Meanwhile, make the salsa. Mix the cherry tomatoes, herbs, capers, remaining 3 tbsp of olive oil, and lemon juice in a bowl and season to taste with salt and pepper.

4. When the lima beans are ready, divide between two plates and spoon the tomato salsa all over. Finish by scattering over the sliced chile and mixed seeds.

Sheet-Pan Harissa Cabbage

15–20g FIBER **6** PLANTS

With its high fiber content, less than five minutes of prep, and hardly any washing up, this dish is perfect for those busy weeknights. You can also adapt or add to the veggies roasted with the cabbage to suit what you have at home—the more the merrier! Make sure the chickpeas are as dry as possible before roasting so they come out nice and crispy. I like to swap the harissa with another condiment like miso or Thai curry paste, depending on my mood.

Method

1. Preheat the oven to 400°F / 200°C. Arrange the vegetables on a large baking sheet and toss with the olive oil, 1 tablespoon of the harissa, and some salt and pepper. Bake in the oven for 35 minutes, turning halfway through, or until the vegetables are soft and browning at the edges and the chickpeas are slightly crispy.

2. Divide the yogurt between two plates and swirl the remaining tablespoon of harissa through it. Top with the roasted vegetables and serve.

Preparation time: 5 minutes
Cook time: 35 minutes

Ingredients (Serves 2 with leftovers)

1 small pointed (sweetheart) cabbage, *sliced into 6 wedges*
1 red onion, *cut into wedges*
1 (14-oz / 400g) can chickpeas, *drained and patted dry*
4½ oz / 130g cherry tomatoes
1 eggplant, *cut into 1-inch / 2.5cm cubes*
2 tbsp extra-virgin olive oil
2 tbsp harissa
6 tbsp / 100g Greek yogurt
Salt and black pepper

Top-ups

Green herbs
Seed Mix Sprinkle (*page 263*)
Savory Crispy Pulses and Grains (*page 267*)

Swaps

Plant-based alternative for Greek yogurt
Any vegetables will work here

Broccoli and Walnut Orecchiette

10–15g **4**
FIBER PLANTS

SATISFYING MAINS

Pasta is a fantastic vehicle for flavor and texture, and this dish is a great example of how combining foods can help your blood sugar response. There's plenty of healthy fats from the walnuts in the delicious and satisfying sauce, as well as fiber from the broccoli—both of which slow your blood sugar response. This is fuss-free, healthy cooking at its finest.

Method

1. Bring a large saucepan of salted water to a boil and cook the pasta for 10 minutes.

2. Meanwhile, put the tomatoes, walnuts, and Boosting Bouillon into a food processor with a pinch of salt and pepper and blend until you have a chunky paste.

3. After the pasta has been cooking for 10 minutes, add the broccoli florets to the pan and cook for 2 minutes longer. Drain, reserving about 6 tbsp / 100ml of the cooking water.

4. Add the walnut and tomato paste to the saucepan along with almost all the reserved pasta water, mix, and heat through for 1 minute. Return the pasta and broccoli to the pan and toss to combine everything. Add a splash more water if needed, season with salt and pepper, and serve.

Preparation time: *10 minutes*
Cook time: *15 minutes*

Ingredients (Serves 2)

3½ oz / 100g orecchiette
1 cup / 150g cherry tomatoes
¾ cup / 80g walnut pieces
2 tbsp Boosting Bouillon
 (page 264) **or nutritional yeast**
1 large head broccoli
 (12 oz / 350g), cut into small florets
Salt and black pepper

Top-up

Nut Crumb *(page 262)*

Swap

Parmesan for Boosting Bouillon

Pantry Raid

178 Always-There Risotto
180 Black Bean "Meat" Balls
184 Pea Soup with Crispy Caper Chickpeas
187 Corn and Spinach Dal
188 Minestrone
191 Artichoke and Sun-Dried Tomato Stew
192 Coconut-Spinach Lentils
195 Anchovy and Artichoke Pasta
196 Braised Beans and Greens

Life's rhythms sometimes take us away from home or the shops. We've all been there: arriving home from vacation, or coming back late after a long day and walking into a kitchen that has been neglected. When we're tired or low on groceries, it's easy to believe a nutritious meal is out of reach. But this is when the foundational contents of your fridge and pantry become the unsung heroes, providing delicious combinations you can create in minutes.

Like me, you probably always have onions, garlic, carrots, and celery lurking in your kitchen. These make a fabulous mirepoix mix, adding a flavorful base of four plants to a recipe. Whenever you have surplus fresh herbs, chop and mix them with olive oil before freezing them in ice-cube trays. This way, you'll always have herbs on hand. And let's not forget the economical and nutritional value of frozen, dried, jarred, and canned foods, which sometimes have better micronutrients than their fresh counterparts. With canned beans in the house, there's always a meal on the horizon, so don't be shy about raiding your pantry.

Always-There Risotto

5–10g FIBER   **4** PLANTS

Risottos can have a reputation for being high-maintenance, but this one is just waiting for you to open your pantry and bring it to life with minimal fuss. The pearl barley has more fiber than rice and diversifies the grains for your gut health. The frozen spinach retains its nutrients really well, but any greens will work here.

Method

1. Preheat the oven to 350°F / 180°C.

2. Put the dried mushrooms in a large bowl and cover with 3½ cups / 800ml boiling water.

3. Heat the olive oil in a medium Dutch oven over medium heat and add the onion. Sauté with a pinch of salt for 5 minutes with the lid on, stirring from time to time. Remove the lid and cook for 3 minutes more, caramelizing the onion to create depth of flavor.

4. Strain the mushrooms, reserving the strained stock, and finely chop them. Add to the Dutch oven along with the mushroom stock, pearl barley, and miso. Mix well and bring to a boil, then cover with a lid and transfer to the oven. Bake for 35 minutes, stirring halfway through.

5. When the risotto is ready, remove from the oven, stir in the defrosted spinach and grated Parmesan, and season with salt and pepper. Return the lid to the dish and allow to rest for 5 minutes before serving.

Preparation time: *10 minutes*
Cook time: *45 minutes*

Ingredients (Serves 2 with leftovers)

1½ oz / 40g dried mushrooms
1 tbsp extra-virgin olive oil
1 onion, *finely chopped*
1 cup / 200g pearl barley
1 tbsp miso
12–14 oz / 350–400g frozen spinach, *defrosted*
1 cup / 30g finely grated Parmesan cheese
Salt and black pepper

Top-ups

Nut Crumb *(page 262)*
Tempeh Crumble *(page 266)*
Sauerkraut *(page 64)*

Swap

2 tbsp nutritional yeast for the Parmesan

Black Bean "Meat" Balls

20–25g FIBER   **9** PLANTS

A symphony of flavors features in these meatless meatballs. The miso brings an umami punch, while the lemon zest brings a pungent acidity and aroma. The black beans join with polyphenols and fiber, while the canned tomatoes bring lycopene to the plate. Serve these with steamed greens, pasta, or lentils.

Method

1. Heat 1 tablespoon of the olive oil in a large nonstick frying pan over medium heat and sauté half the chopped onions for 5 minutes, stirring occasionally, until soft. Add 1 of the chopped garlic cloves and cook for 1 minute more.

2. Transfer to a blender or food processor with the canned tomatoes, basil, vinegar, and miso and blend until smooth. Set aside.

3. Return the frying pan to medium heat, add another tablespoon of oil, and sauté the remaining onions with the carrot and celery for 5 minutes, stirring occasionally, until the vegetables have softened. Add the remaining chopped garlic and cook for 1 minute more.

4. Transfer to a food processor with the black beans, walnuts, lemon zest, and herbs (if using). Season with salt and pepper and process to combine. Once the mixture has clumped together, stop processing to keep some texture from the nuts and beans.

5. Shape the mixture tightly into 12 firm balls, roughly the size of a golf ball—damp hands will help here. Chill the balls in the fridge for 2 hours to firm them up. (If you don't have 2 hours to spare, just take extra care when cooking.)

6. Add the remaining 2 tablespoons of olive oil to the frying pan and place over medium heat. Gently fry the balls on all sides until they have taken on a bit of color—this should only take 6 minutes. Pour in the tomato sauce, spreading it around the balls, and simmer for another 4–5 minutes.

Preparation time: 20 minutes, plus 2 hours chilling
Cook time: 25 minutes

Ingredients (Serves 3–4)

- 4 tbsp extra-virgin olive oil
- 2 small onions, *finely chopped*
- 4 garlic cloves, *finely chopped*
- 1 (14-oz / 400g) can diced tomatoes
- 2 tbsp fresh or frozen basil
- 1 tsp apple cider vinegar
- 2 tbsp miso
- 1 carrot, *finely diced*
- 1 celery stalk, *finely diced*
- 1 (14-oz / 400g) can black beans, *drained*
- 2¾ oz / 80g walnuts (⅔ cup chopped)
- Zest of 1 lemon
- Fresh, frozen, or dried herbs (optional)
- Salt and black pepper

Top-ups

Seed Mix Sprinkle (page 263)
Sauerkraut (page 64)
Basil

Swap

Kidney beans for black beans

PANTRY RAID

Pea Soup with Crispy Caper Chickpeas

10–15g FIBER **6** PLANTS

PANTRY RAID

This is a really satisfying soup that only takes 25 minutes to make (assuming you cook the soup while the chickpeas are roasting). The crispy capers and the chickpeas make a fantastic snack on their own. You can also add them to other dishes as a top-up.

Method

1. Preheat the oven to 425°F / 220°C and line a baking sheet with parchment paper.

2. Toss the chickpeas with 1 tablespoon of the olive oil, season with salt and pepper, and spread out on the baking sheet. Roast in the oven for 10 minutes. Carefully remove the sheet from the oven and add the capers. Stir to combine and return to the oven for 10–15 minutes, until the capers and chickpeas are crispy and bursting open.

3. Heat the remaining tablespoon of olive oil in a saucepan over medium heat and sauté the onion and celery for 4–5 minutes, until softened and turning golden. Meanwhile, bring 3½ cups/ 800ml of water to the boil. Add the boiling water to the saucepan and cook for 3 minutes to further soften the onion and celery.

4. Add the peas, miso, and chiles and simmer for 5 minutes. Remove from the heat, allow to cool slightly, then season and process until smooth.

5. Serve topped with the crispy chickpeas and capers, a drizzle of olive oil, and the brine from the chiles for acidity.

Preparation time: *5 minutes*
Cook time: *20–25 minutes*

Ingredients (Serves 4)

1 (14-oz / 400g) can chickpeas, *drained and patted dry*
2 tbsp extra-virgin olive oil, *plus extra for drizzling*
4 tbsp capers
1 onion, *finely chopped*
2 celery stalks, *finely chopped*
4¼ cups / 550g frozen peas
1 tbsp miso
4 pickled green chiles, *coarsely chopped, plus 1 tbsp of their brine*
Salt and black pepper

Top-ups

Kefir
Fresh or frozen herbs
Seed Mix Sprinkle *(page 263)*

Swap

2 tbsp Boosting Bouillon *(page 264) for miso*

5–10g
FIBER

12
PLANTS

Corn and Spinach Dal

Preparation time: *10 minutes*
Cook time: *30 minutes*

Ingredients *(Serves 4)*

2 (7-oz / 195g) cans corn and their liquid
4 tbsp extra-virgin olive oil
1 onion, *finely chopped*
3 garlic cloves, *finely chopped*
1 tsp ground turmeric
1 tsp ground coriander
1 tsp garam masala
1½ tsp chile flakes
¾ cup / 160g split red lentils
6¼ oz / 160g frozen spinach
2 tbsp cumin seeds
1 tbsp dried curry leaves
   (optional)
Salt and black pepper

Top-ups

Soft-boiled egg
Fresh chile, chopped or sliced
Cilantro

Swap

Fresh spinach for frozen
   (add at the end to wilt)

This is a great moment to incorporate those half-used bags of grains in the back of your pantry. Simply add them to the dal while cooking (making sure you extend the cooking time to the grain that takes the longest to cook), and you'll have even more plants in your dish; plus you'll be reducing food waste. The wide range of spices likewise adds polyphenols that are great for your gut health. Feel free to use fresh or frozen corn instead of canned if that's what you have on hand—you may just need to add a little extra water.

Method

1. Empty 1 can of corn and its liquid into a blender, add 2⅓ cups / 550ml of water, and blend until smooth.

2. Heat 2 tablespoons of the olive oil in a saucepan over medium heat and sauté the onion for 3 minutes, until soft and translucent. Add the garlic and cook for 30 seconds more.

3. Add the spices and cook for 30 seconds, then stir in the lentils, frozen spinach, blended corn stock, and the remaining can of corn and its liquid. Bring to a boil, then lower the heat and simmer gently for 15–20 minutes, or until the lentils are soft. Add a dash of water if the dal becomes too thick. Season generously with salt and pepper.

4. Just before the dal finishes cooking, heat the remaining 2 tablespoons of olive oil in a small frying pan and add the cumin seeds and curry leaves (if using). Cook over low to medium heat for 1 minute, until the seeds start to pop. Pour over the dal, stir to combine, and serve.

Minestrone

10–15g FIBER   **7** PLANTS

When you have odds and ends to use up in your fridge, this minestrone base will be your go-to recipe, giving you a head start on the plant count with its classic mirepoix base of onion, carrots, and celery, plus garlic. The plant fiber will help moderate your blood sugar response from the pasta, and the sun-dried tomatoes add a delicious depth of flavor. If you're adding a lot more vegetables, adjust the recipe to incorporate a little more liquid.

Preparation time: *10 minutes*
Cook time: *35 minutes*

Ingredients (Serves 4)

2 tbsp extra-virgin olive oil
1 onion, *coarsely chopped*
2 celery stalks, *coarsely chopped*
2 carrots, *peeled and coarsely chopped*
3 garlic cloves, *coarsely chopped*
14 oz / 400g fresh or canned diced tomatoes
1¾ cups / 100g sun-dried tomatoes, *coarsely chopped*
1 (14-oz / 400g) can cannellini beans and their liquid
2 tbsp Boosting Bouillon (page 264)
1¾ oz / 50g ditalini or any other small pasta
Salt and black pepper

Method

1. Heat the olive oil in a large saucepan over medium heat, add the onion, celery, and carrots and sauté for 10 minutes, stirring occasionally. Add the garlic and cook for 1 minute more.

2. Add the fresh or canned tomatoes, sun-dried tomatoes, canned beans and their liquid, the Boosting Bouillon, pasta, and 1½ cans of water, adding more liquid as needed. Simmer gently for 25 minutes.

3. Taste and season before serving. The minestrone will keep for up to 4 days in the fridge and will get better each day. The minestrone will thicken slightly as it cools, so you may need to add a little more water when reheating.

Top-ups

Frozen vegetables
Basil
Capers

Swaps

Stock cube for Boosting Bouillon
Any beans for cannellini

10–15g
FIBER

11
PLANTS

Artichoke and Sun-Dried Tomato Stew

Preparation time: *15 minutes*
Cook time: *20 minutes*

Ingredients (Serves 4)

2 tbsp extra-virgin olive oil
1 onion, *finely chopped*
1 carrot, *peeled and cut into ⅜-inch / 1cm dice*
3 garlic cloves, *chopped*
1 (14-oz / 400g) can diced tomatoes
1½ tbsp harissa
1 (14-oz / 400g) can cranberry beans and their liquid
2 tbsp Boosting Bouillon *(optional; page 264)*
1 (10-oz / 285g) jar artichokes, *drained and coarsely chopped (5¾ oz / 160g drained weight)*
1½ cups / 80g sun-dried tomatoes, *coarsely chopped*
Scant ½ cup / 75g pitted olives
7 oz / 200g frozen green beans *(or a 7-oz / 200g mix of any green vegetables from your freezer or fridge)*
Juice of ½ lemon
Salt and black pepper

Top-up

Mixed ACV Pickles *(page 269)*

Swap

Stock cube for Boosting Bouillon

A delicious casserole is just the thing when you're after something substantial. Jarred artichokes are a handy way to add prebiotics to a meal, satisfying your gut bacteria. Olives bring flavor and fiber, and the lemon juice adds a delightful acidity to your plate while helping your body absorb the iron from the beans.

Method

1. Heat the olive oil in a large Dutch oven over medium heat and sauté the onion and carrot for 4 minutes, stirring occasionally, until the onion has softened. Add the garlic and cook for 1 minute more.

2. Add the canned tomatoes, harissa, cranberry beans and their liquid, the Boosting Bouillon (if using), artichokes, sun-dried tomatoes, and olives. Simmer, covered, for 10 minutes.

3. Stir in the frozen green beans and cook, covered, for 3–4 minutes longer, until the beans are tender. Add the lemon juice just before serving and season with a generous pinch of salt and pepper.

Coconut-Spinach Lentils

5–10g FIBER **11** PLANTS

The warming spices in this recipe bring the plant score up to 11, while the coconut milk is suitable for those avoiding dairy, and has the benefit of a long shelf life. Lentils and cashews bring protein and fiber, making this a satisfying dish conjured from your pantry.

Method

1. Heat the olive oil in a saucepan, add the onion, and sauté over medium heat for 4 minutes, until softened, stirring occasionally. Add the garlic and cook for 30 seconds more.

2. Stir in all the spices and cook for 30 seconds, then pour the coconut milk and the lentils and their liquid into the saucepan. Half fill one of the empty cans with water and add this to the curry. Reduce the heat and leave to simmer for 10 minutes, until slightly thickened.

3. Add the Boosting Bouillon, frozen spinach, and cashews and simmer for a further 8 minutes, stirring to encourage the frozen spinach to defrost and separate. Taste, season with salt and pepper, and serve.

Preparation time: *5 minutes*
Cook time: *25 minutes*

Ingredients (Serves 4)

2 tbsp extra-virgin olive oil
1 onion, *sliced*
2 garlic cloves, *coarsely chopped*
1 tbsp cumin seeds
1 tbsp garam masala
1 tsp ground turmeric
1 tsp chile powder
1 (14-oz / 400ml) can coconut milk
1 (14-oz / 400g) can green lentils and their liquid
2 tbsp Boosting Bouillon (page 264)
10 oz / 300g frozen spinach
Scant 1 cup / 130g cashews
Salt and black pepper

Top-ups

Tofu
Pearls and Puy (page 265)
Fresh chile, chopped or sliced

Swap

Canned beans for canned lentils

15–20g **7**
FIBER   PLANTS

Anchovy and Artichoke Pasta

Preparation time: *5 minutes*
Cook time: *15 minutes*

Ingredients (Serves 2)

3½ oz / 100g whole-wheat penne or fusilli
2 tbsp extra-virgin olive oil
2 garlic cloves, *finely chopped*
2–5 canned anchovy fillets
   (to taste), coarsely chopped
1 tsp chile flakes
1 (14-oz / 400g) can chickpeas and their liquid
1 (10-oz / 285g) jar artichokes, *drained and coarsely chopped (5¾ oz / 160g drained weight)*
1½ cups / 200g frozen peas
Zest and juice of ½ lemon
Salt and black pepper

Top-up

Seed Mix Sprinkle *(page 263)*

Swap

Capers for anchovy fillets

Anchovies are a bit like Marmite, so if they're not to your taste, you can swap them for capers, which will add their own punchy, umami taste to this dish. The chickpeas and peas are full of fiber, which will moderate your blood sugar response to the pasta, and the artichokes bring prebiotics to delight your gut bacteria.

Method

1. Cook the pasta in a saucepan of salted water for 8 minutes, until al dente, then drain and set aside.

2. Heat the olive oil in a frying pan and sauté the garlic over low heat for 1 minute. Stir in the anchovies and chile flakes and cook for 30 seconds more.

3. Add the chickpeas and their liquid along with the cooked pasta. Increase the heat and simmer for 2–3 minutes, until the anchovies have melted into the sauce and the liquid has reduced by half.

4. Add the artichokes, peas, and lemon zest and juice and cook for 3 minutes more, until the vegetables are heated through. Season with salt and pepper and serve.

Braised Beans and Greens

PANTRY RAID

You can use any white beans here, but we've used a mix of cannellini, lima beans, and navy beans for extra diversity. Add any frozen or fresh greens you have on hand—just be sure to match the quantity to 18 oz / 500g. Parmesan cheese adds probiotics, but if you want to make this vegan, you can swap it for nutritional yeast and add sauerkraut instead.

Method

1. Heat the olive oil in a large Dutch oven and sauté the onion over medium heat for 3 minutes, stirring occasionally. Add the garlic and chile flakes and cook for 30 seconds more.

2. Pour in all the beans with their liquid and add the miso and the frozen green vegetables. Mix everything together and simmer for 3–4 minutes, until everything is just cooked.

3. Stir in almost all the Parmesan and season with a pinch of salt and pepper. Serve topped with the remaining Parmesan and a drizzle of olive oil.

10–15g FIBER   **8** PLANTS

Preparation time: *5 minutes*
Cook time: *10 minutes*

Ingredients (Serves 4)

2 tbsp extra-virgin olive oil, *plus extra for drizzling*
1 onion, *finely chopped*
3 garlic cloves, *finely chopped*
½ tsp chile flakes
1 (14-oz / 400g) can cannellini beans and their liquid
1 (14-oz / 400g) can lima beans and their liquid
1 (14-oz / 400g) can navy beans and their liquid
1 tbsp miso
18 oz / 500g mix of frozen green vegetables, such as spinach, peas, fava beans, green beans
1 oz / 30g grated Parmesan cheese
Salt and black pepper

Top-ups

Nut Crumb *(page 262)*
Sauerkraut *(page 64)*

Swap

2 tbsp nutritional yeast for Parmesan cheese

Entertaining

200 Sheet-Pan Roasted Eggplant

203 Juno's Lasagna

204 Roasted Squash with Toasted Grains

209 Mushroom and Leek Tart

210 Black Bean Chili

212 Harissa-Hazelnut Roast

215 Whole Roast Cauliflower

216 Bulgur with Aioli

The parts of the world where communal eating is common, like Sardinia, Ikaria, or Okinawa, have increased longevity and less metabolic disease. These areas, called the Blue Zones, have the highest concentration of healthy centenarians, suggesting that the social aspect of eating together may contribute to a longer, healthier life. Data from national surveys in the UK also shows that those who often eat socially feel happier, are more satisfied with life, and are more engaged in their communities. Sharing a table or a dish with others can improve overall well-being and happiness, and it creates a sense of community and belonging, which are important factors for mental health.

To foster that connection, we've created these recipes for you to share the joy of eating well with your friends and family. Treat these dishes as the centerpiece of your table and make a beautiful spread along with the vibrant salads and other recipes in this book—or sides of fish or meat if you prefer.

Sheet-Pan Roasted Eggplant

10–15g FIBER   **13** PLANTS

Sheet-pan dishes are so simple to make, but the garnishes here make it look like a showstopper and bring the plant score up to 13, giving you plenty of polyphenols and a boost of fiber. The best entertaining recipes require very little active time in the kitchen, and this one fills the bill. Prepare the baking sheets for baking in advance and pop them in the oven 40 minutes before serving.

Method

1. Preheat the oven to 400°F / 200°C and line two large baking sheets with parchment paper.

2. Put the chickpeas, tomatoes, peppers, halloumi, and garlic on one sheet with three-quarters each of the cumin, coriander, and chile powder. Season with salt and pepper and drizzle with 3 tablespoons of the olive oil. Toss to coat.

3. Cut each eggplant in half lengthwise and score a ¾-inch / 2cm-deep criss-cross pattern into the flesh of each piece. Sprinkle with the remaining ground spices and drizzle with the remaining tablespoon of olive oil, season with salt and pepper, and place on the other baking sheet. Place both sheets in the oven for 40 minutes.

4. Make a sauce: mix the tahini, kefir, and sumac in a bowl and season with salt and pepper. When the vegetables are roasted, squeeze the garlic cloves from their peels into the sauce, mash them in, and stir to combine.

5. Transfer the chickpeas, halloumi, and vegetables to a serving dish and stir in three-quarters of the cilantro. Place the eggplant halves on top and scatter with the remaining cilantro, green onions, pomegranate seeds, lime juice, and the sauce.

Preparation time: 15 minutes
Cook time: 40 minutes

Ingredients (Serves 4)

2 (14-oz / 400g) cans chickpeas, drained and patted dry
2¼ cups / 350g cherry tomatoes
2 bell peppers, cut into ¾-inch / 2cm chunks
7 oz / 200g halloumi, cut into ⅜-inch / 1cm cubes
3 garlic cloves, unpeeled
2½ tsp ground cumin
1½ tsp ground coriander
1 tsp chile powder
4 tbsp extra-virgin olive oil
2 eggplants
3 tbsp tahini
¾ cup / 180ml kefir
2 tsp sumac
¾ oz / 20g cilantro, coarsely chopped
4 green onions, thinly sliced
3 tbsp pomegranate seeds
Juice of 1 lime
Salt and black pepper

Top-ups

Savory Crispy Pulses and Grains (page 267)
Sauerkraut (page 64)

Swaps

Firm tofu for halloumi
Plant-based yogurt for kefir

10–15g FIBER **13** PLANTS

Juno's Lasagna

Preparation time: *30 minutes*
Cook time: *1½ hours*

Ingredients (Serves 8)

1½ oz / 40g dried porcini mushrooms
3 tbsp extra-virgin olive oil
12 oz / 350g cremini mushrooms, *finely chopped*
1 onion, *finely chopped*
2 carrots, *finely diced*
1 celery stalk, *finely diced*
3 garlic cloves, *finely chopped*
1¼ cups / 70g sun-dried tomatoes, *thinly sliced*
1 (14-oz / 400g) can green lentils and their liquid
3 cups / 690ml passata or tomato purée
2 tsp miso
1⅔ cups lightly packed / 20g basil, *sliced in chiffonade*
1 (14-oz / 400g) can cannellini beans, *drained (reserve 5 tbsp liquid)*
5¼ oz / 150g silken tofu
¼ tsp grated nutmeg
9 sheets whole-wheat lasagna noodles (5¾ oz / 160g)
1½ cups / 200g grated Cheddar or cheese of choice *(or a plant-based alternative)*
Salt and black pepper

Swap

Any white beans for cannellini

Nobody forgets their favorite childhood dish, and this is mine: a reimagining of my mother Juno's lasagna using lots of delicious veggies. Canned cannellini beans, silken tofu, miso, and nutmeg make up the béchamel, adding even more fiber to the dish. Passata is puréed tomatoes seasoned with salt only; tomato purée in cans or a carton is a fine equivalent.

Method

1. Preheat the oven to 375°F / 190°C. Pour 1½ cups / 350ml of boiling water over the dried mushrooms and set aside.

2. Place a large heavy pan (one with a lid) over high heat with the olive oil and sauté the cremini mushrooms with a pinch of salt for 6–8 minutes, until they're turning golden.

3. Reduce the heat to medium, then add the onion, carrots, and celery along with 2 tablespoons of water. Cover and sweat for 8 minutes, stirring occasionally. Add the garlic and cook, covered, for 2 minutes more.

4. Add the sun-dried tomatoes, lentils and their liquid, the passata, and miso, mixing to combine. Drain the mushrooms with a sieve placed over a bowl, add the soaking liquid to the pan, and finely chop the mushrooms before adding these to the pan too. Stir, season generously with salt and pepper, and simmer with the lid on for 10 minutes. Add the basil and simmer for 5 minutes more, then taste and adjust the seasoning.

5. Pour the cannellini beans and the 5 tablespoons of the reserved liquid into a blender with the tofu and nutmeg, then blend until completely smooth. Season generously with salt and pepper.

6. To assemble, spoon a third of the lentil ragu into a 9 x 11-inch / 23 x 27cm rectangular baking dish. Top with 3 sheets of lasagna, a third of the cannellini béchamel, and 2 tablespoons of cheese. Repeat twice more, then top with the remaining cheese. Bake in the oven for 40–50 minutes, until the lasagna is bubbling and the cheese golden.

Roasted Squash with Toasted Grains

10–15g FIBER **8** PLANTS

Once you toast grains like this in the oven, you won't look back—it's the best topping to add texture to your meals. The relish adds a bright freshness, contrasting well with the sweet, soft squash, and you can add any other seasonal vegetables to the recipe that you have on hand, like roasted beets or celeriac.

Preparation time: *15 minutes*
Cook time: *45 minutes*

Method

1. Preheat the oven to 375°F / 190°C and line a large baking sheet with parchment paper.

2. Place the squash and garlic on the lined baking sheet, drizzle with 2 tablespoons of the olive oil, and season well. Roast for 35 minutes.

3. Take the sheet out of the oven and remove and set aside the garlic cloves. Scatter the precooked grains over the squash and return to the oven for 10–15 minutes, until the grains are crispy and the squash is soft.

4. Squeeze the cooked garlic cloves from their skins into a high-powered blender with the beans and their liquid, the tahini, and the lemon juice. Season and blend until completely smooth.

5. Mix the parsley, olives, apple cider vinegar, and remaining 2 tablespoons of olive oil in a bowl and season. To serve, spread the puréed cannellini beans over the bottom of a large serving dish, top with the squash and grains, and scatter over the parsley and olive relish.

Ingredients *(Serves 4)*

1 large winter squash, *seeded, skin on, and cut into 1-inch- / 2.5cm-thick slices*
2 garlic cloves, *unpeeled*
4 tbsp extra-virgin olive oil
1⅓ cups / 250g precooked mixed grains
1 (14-oz / 400g) can cannellini beans and their liquid
2 tbsp tahini
Juice of 1 lemon
1⅔ cups / 20g lightly packed parsley, *finely chopped*
⅓ cup / 50g green olives, *finely chopped*
2 tbsp apple cider vinegar
Salt and black pepper

Top-ups

Chopped red chile
Sauerkraut *(page 64)*
Nut Crumb *(page 262)*

Swap

Any white beans for cannellini

ENTERTAINING

<5g
FIBER

7
PLANTS

Mushroom and Leek Tart

Preparation time: 20 minutes
Cook time: 40 minutes

Ingredients (Serves 6–8)

2 cups / 255g whole-grain spelt flour, *plus extra for dusting*
⅓ cup / 80ml extra-virgin olive oil, *plus 2 tbsp*
8½ oz / 250g mushrooms, *sliced (use a mix of varieties, if possible)*
3 leeks, *halved and thinly sliced*
4 green onions, *thinly sliced*
½ cup / 65g frozen peas
1 cup / 10g fresh dill, *finely chopped*
6 tbsp / 50g coarsely chopped walnuts
1 cup / 250g Greek yogurt
4 eggs
2 tbsp grated Cheddar cheese
Salt and black pepper

Top-up

Sauerkraut *(page 64)*

Swap

Pumpkin or sunflower seeds for walnuts

Tarts are perfect for sharing alfresco, and this one uses one of my favorite ingredients: mushrooms. Their health benefits are vast, and they come in a great variety, increasing your plant-food diversity. Using spelt flour here adds extra fiber to the crust.

Method

1. Preheat the oven to 400°F / 200°C. Put the flour, the ⅓ cup / 80ml of olive oil, and ½ cup / 125ml water into a bowl with a pinch of salt and pepper and mix to combine. It may look wet, but it comes together into a soft dough that will feel a little oily. Knead gently on a lightly floured surface until smooth, no more than 1 minute, then wrap in parchment paper and refrigerate for 10 minutes.

2. Grease a deep 9-inch / 23cm tart pan with a little olive oil and dust with flour. Transfer the pastry to a floured work surface and roll out to a circle that is 1 inch / 2.5cm larger than the pan. Carefully transfer the pastry to the pan (it will help to roll the pastry around the rolling pin), then press it into the sides and trim the edges. Prick the bottom with a fork and bake in the oven for 12 minutes, until the pastry is dry to the touch and crisp, but not colored, around the edges.

3. Meanwhile, heat 1 tablespoon of olive oil in a large frying pan and sauté the mushrooms over medium heat for 3–4 minutes. Season with salt and pepper and transfer to a large bowl. Add the remaining tablespoon of olive oil to the pan and sauté the leeks for 5 minutes, until softened.

4. Transfer the leeks to the bowl with the mushrooms, allow to cool slightly, then add the green onions, peas, dill, walnuts, yogurt, and eggs. Mix until well combined, then season with salt and pepper.

5. Pour the mixture into the tart shell and scatter with the cheese. Bake for 30 minutes, or until set.

Black Bean Chili

5–10g FIBER **10** PLANTS

This is a versatile recipe for entertaining: you can pile this chili into a baked potato or onto homemade flatbreads, or serve it with eggs and avocado for a huevos rancheros–inspired breakfast. I think black beans are a much undervalued source of plant protein, fiber, and polyphenols and—crucially—they're delicious!

Method

1. Heat 2 tablespoons of the olive oil in a saucepan and sauté the onion over medium heat for 5 minutes until softened. Add the garlic and cook for 1 minute more. Stir in the spices and cook for 30 seconds.

2. Add the diced tomatoes, black beans and their liquid, and a generous pinch of salt and pepper, and simmer for 15 minutes, or until the sauce has thickened and is coating the beans. Allow to cool slightly, then add half the lime juice and half the cilantro.

3. Toss the tomatoes, lime zest, remaining cilantro, lime juice, and olive oil together in a bowl and season with salt and pepper.

4. Serve the chili with the cherry tomatoes alongside.

Preparation time: *15 minutes*
Cook time: *25 minutes*

Ingredients (Serves 4)

3 tbsp extra-virgin olive oil
1 onion, *finely chopped*
2 garlic cloves, *finely chopped*
1 tsp cumin
1 tsp paprika
1 tsp chile flakes
1 (14-oz / 400g) can diced tomatoes
1 (14-oz / 400g) can black beans and their liquid
Zest and juice of 1 lime
2 cups / 40g tightly packed cilantro, *coarsely chopped*
2¼ cups / 350g cherry tomatoes, *quartered*
Salt and black pepper

Top-ups

Sour cream or yogurt
Avocado
Pearls and Puy *(page 265)*

Harissa-Hazelnut Roast

5–10g FIBER   **13** PLANTS

This wonderfully moist and flavorful nut roast comes with a packed plant score of 13 and makes a fantastic centerpiece for special occasions like Christmas or for a gathering with family and friends. Make the sauce vegan by swapping the Greek yogurt for a plant-based one.

Method

1. Mix the flaxseed meal with 6 tablespoons of tepid water and set aside. This will form a "flax egg," which can be used later as an egg substitute. Preheat the oven to 375°F / 190°C and line a 2-lb / 900g loaf pan with parchment paper.

2. Heat the olive oil in a large frying pan over low heat and add the onion, carrot, and celery. Stir to combine, cover, and sweat the vegetables for 10 minutes to soften. Add the garlic and cook for 1 minute longer.

3. Add the mushrooms and sauté for 10–12 minutes, until they have softened and all their liquid has evaporated. Stir in the harissa, season with salt and pepper, allow to cool slightly, and transfer to a food processor along with the hazelnuts. Blend until almost smooth, then transfer to a bowl.

4. Add the flax egg, almond meal, and lime zest and juice to the mushroom paste. Mix to combine and then transfer to the prepared pan. Press the mixture down firmly and bake for 40 minutes, until firm. When ready, cool in the pan for 10 minutes to firm up, then slice.

5. Meanwhile, mix the yogurt and tahini together in a bowl. Add a few tablespoons of cold water and mix until you have the consistency of cream; season with salt and pepper. Serve each slice of nut roast drizzled with the tahini sauce and topped with pomegranate seeds.

Preparation time: 25 minutes
Cook time: 1 hour

Ingredients (Serves 6)

- 3 tbsp flaxseed meal
- 2 tbsp extra-virgin olive oil
- 1 onion, *finely chopped*
- 1 carrot, *finely chopped*
- 1 celery stalk, *finely chopped*
- 3 garlic cloves, *finely chopped*
- 1 lb / 450g cremini mushrooms, *finely chopped*
- 3 tbsp harissa
- 2 cups / 250g hazelnuts
- 6½ tbsp / 50g almond meal or flour
- Zest and juice of 1 lime
- ¾ cup / 185g Greek yogurt
- 3 tbsp tahini
- ½ cup / 80g pomegranate seeds
- Salt and black pepper

Top-up

Steamed greens

Swap

Plant-based yogurt for Greek yogurt

20–25g **11**
FIBER PLANTS

Whole Roast Cauliflower

Preparation time: *25 minutes*
Cook time: *1–1½ hours*

Ingredients (Serves 4–6)

1 large cauliflower, *stalk and leaves attached*
6 tbsp extra-virgin olive oil
1½ oz / 40g mix of herbs, *finely chopped*
4 pickled green chiles, *finely chopped*
2 tbsp capers, *finely chopped*
Scant ½ cup / 60g pistachios, *finely chopped*
2 tbsp apple cider vinegar
1 onion, *finely chopped*
2 garlic cloves, *finely chopped*
3 (14-oz / 400g) cans lima beans and their liquid
½ cup / 60g frozen peas
2 tbsp tahini
1 tbsp miso
1 recipe Kefir Dressing *(page 271)*
Salt and black pepper

Top-ups

Sauerkraut *(page 64)*
Fried garlic slices

Swap

Pumpkin seeds or pecans for pistachios

The humble cauliflower takes center stage here, accompanied by a plethora of fantastic herbs, such as parsley, mint, or chives. This is such an easy meal to make for guests, and is one that will satisfy them with lots of flavors and textures, with the pistachios adding a pleasing crunch. Swap the kefir in the dressing for a plant-based yogurt to make it vegan.

Method

1. Preheat the oven to 350°F / 180°C. Slice the base of the cauliflower so it will stand upright. Bring a large saucepan of water to a boil and simmer the cauliflower upside down for 5 minutes. Drain in a colander, leaving it to steam for 5 minutes. Transfer to a roasting pan, right side up; drizzle 2 tablespoons of the olive oil all over and season. Roast for 1–1½ hours, until golden brown and tender when pierced with a sharp knife.

2. Meanwhile, mix the chopped herbs, green chiles, capers, and pistachios together in a bowl. Add the apple cider vinegar and 2 tablespoons of the olive oil and season with salt and pepper.

3. Heat the remaining 2 tablespoons of olive oil in a large frying pan over medium heat and sauté the onion for 5 minutes, until softened. Add the garlic and cook for 1 minute more.

4. Pour in the beans and their liquid, bring to a simmer, and cook for 8 minutes, until the liquid has thickened and reduced slightly. Add the peas, tahini, and miso and stir to combine, then season to taste and remove from the heat. Allow to cool slightly before stirring in the Kefir Dressing.

5. When the cauliflower is ready, serve on top of the beans, scattered with the herb topping.

Bulgur with Aioli

5–10g FIBER **11** PLANTS

Compared with traditional paellas, this reimagined version is super quick to put together. It's perfect for entertaining. The vegan aioli is smooth and silky, making it the star topping to the dish. When the heat is turned off, the bulgur wheat will absorb the liquid, so letting it rest is an important step. Serve this with a salad, veggies, seafood, or a meat dish of your choice.

Method

1. Put the saffron and sun-dried tomatoes into a jug and cover with 1¼ cups / 300ml boiling water to make a stock. Add 1 teaspoon salt and a generous pinch of pepper.

2. Put a large, lidded Dutch oven (12 inches / 30cm in diameter or similar) over medium heat, add 2 tablespoons of the olive oil, and sauté the leek and rosemary for 3–4 minutes, until softened. Add three-quarters of the garlic and cook for 1 minute more.

3. Stir in the paprika and cayenne, then add the green beans, broccolini, and chopped roasted red peppers. Add about 4 tablespoons of water—it will sizzle and steam. Immediately place a tight-fitting lid on top and let the veggies steam for 3–4 minutes.

4. Scatter the bulgur all over the vegetables and pour in the saffron stock. Give the pan a shake to disperse the liquid and bulgur evenly, then lay the sliced red pepper on top. Simmer for 5 minutes, then turn off the heat, return the lid, and leave for 15 minutes, or until all the water is absorbed.

5. To make the aioli, blitz the tofu, lemon juice, the remaining garlic, and the remaining 2 tablespoons of olive oil until smooth and season with salt and pepper. When the dish is ready, serve topped with spoonfuls of tofu aioli.

Preparation time: *15 minutes*
Cook time: *30 minutes*

Ingredients (Serves 4)

Pinch of saffron
4 sun-dried tomatoes, *finely chopped*
4 tbsp extra-virgin olive oil
1 leek, *thinly sliced*
2 sprigs rosemary, *leaves picked and chopped*
3 garlic cloves, *finely chopped*
2 tsp smoked paprika
½ tsp cayenne pepper
8 oz / 225g green beans
4 oz / 120g broccolini, *coarsely chopped*
4 roasted red peppers from a jar, *3 chopped and 1 sliced into 6 pieces*
1¼ cups / 200g bulgur
4 oz / 120g silken tofu
Juice of 1 lemon
Salt and black pepper

Top-ups

Olives
Parsley

Swaps

Broccoli or purple sprouting broccoli for broccolini
Jarred artichokes for green beans

Sweet Treats

- 221 Pecan Chocolate Cookies
- 222 Beety Brownies
- 224 Lemon Pistachio Loaf
- 226 Chocolate–Olive Oil Mousse
- 230 Carrot Cake with Tahini-Orange Frosting
- 232 Chia-Lemon Pots de Crème
- 234 Mixed Berry Clafouti
- 237 Apple Pecan Strudel
- 238 Raspberry-Granola Crumble
- 240 Berry "Nice" Cream

Enjoying foods that bring us pleasure is such an important part of a healthy relationship with food. Who doesn't love a good dessert after a meal with friends? Making these desserts yourself means that you can add so many wonderful things to your plate. And if you didn't know already, good-quality dark chocolate can be great for your health. It's packed with polyphenols and has more fiber than you might realize. Be sure to look for a dark chocolate with a minimum cocoa content of 70% and no added artificial ingredients for the best health profile.

You'll also notice we use sugar in this chapter. You may be surprised to learn that sugar alternatives, such as coconut sugar or maple syrup, have largely the same effect as white sugar on the body and are much more expensive. Where we suggest sugar, we also add other nutritious ingredients that pack in flavor, fiber, fat, and protein to make those sweet moments another opportunity to nourish your body and your gut. You'll find plenty of fruit, veggies, nuts, and spices in these recipes, just like in the other chapters, so indulge, enjoy, and feel great.

<5g
FIBER

4
PLANTS

Pecan Chocolate Cookies

Preparation time: *10 minutes (plus 15 minutes standing time for the flax egg)*

Cook time: *10–12 minutes*

Ingredients (Makes 12 cookies)

2 tbsp ground flaxseed meal
3 tbsp light brown sugar
¼ cup extra-virgin olive oil
1⅔ cups / 200g almond meal or flour
Scant ½ cup/ 50g chopped pecans
2¾ oz / 80g dark chocolate *(at least 70% cocoa solids), coarsely chopped*
Pinch of salt

Swap

Pumpkin or sunflower seeds for pecans

These cookies are a ZOE favorite on our Instagram. They're a great alternative to ultra-processed snacks, as they're really easy to make and require minimal ingredients. The nuts and olive oil help moderate your blood sugar response, but you can also add other fillings such as oats and raisins. If you like a chewy cookie, take them out of the oven a little early.

Method

1. Preheat the oven to 350°F / 180°C and line a baking sheet with parchment paper. To make the flax egg, mix the flaxseed meal with ¼ cup of water and set aside for 15 minutes.

2. Mix the brown sugar, olive oil, and flax egg together in a bowl. Add the almond meal, pecans, chocolate, and salt and mix again.

3. Shape into 12 tight balls and flatten slightly into cookies about ½-inch / 1cm thick (it helps if you do this with damp hands). Bake for 10–15 minutes, until tinged golden brown at the edges or along the bottom, then leave to cool completely on the baking sheet. Store in an airtight container.

Beety Brownies

<5g FIBER **4** PLANTS

For me, the perfect brownie should be crispy on top and fudgy on the inside, and this ZOE version hits the mark. While adding beets may seem unusual, its flavor and texture combine with the chocolate to make these brownies so delicious, while adding to the plant score. This recipe also works well as a cake for celebrations and is even more delicious served with yogurt and raspberries.

Method

1. Preheat the oven to 350°F / 180°C and line an 8-inch / 23cm square baking pan with parchment paper.

2. Melt the chocolate in a heatproof bowl set over a saucepan of simmering water (making sure the bowl doesn't touch the water). Remove from the heat and set aside.

3. Process the beet into a purée in a food processor.

4. In a large bowl, whisk together the brown sugar and olive oil followed by the slightly cooled melted chocolate. Add the beet purée and stir to combine.

5. Whisk the eggs and beat into the mixture, followed by the almond meal, baking powder, salt, and cocoa powder and stir until combined.

6. Pour into the prepared pan, spread out with a spatula, and sprinkle over the slivered almonds. Bake for 50–60 minutes, or until the brownies are cooked but still fudgy. Wait until it is completely cooled before slicing into 12 squares.

Preparation time: *10 minutes*
Cook time: *45 minutes*

Ingredients (Serves 12)

3 oz / 90g dark chocolate (at least 70% cocoa solids)
10 oz / 280g precooked beet (use vacuum-packed for ease)
¾ cup packed / 150g dark brown sugar
¾ cup / 200ml extra-virgin olive oil
3 medium eggs
1⅔ cups / 200g almond meal or flour
1 tsp baking powder
Pinch of salt
1 heaped tbsp cocoa powder
½ cup / 60g slivered almonds

Top-ups

Serve with raspberries and yogurt

Swaps

Any nuts or a drizzle of tahini for slivered almonds

Lemon Pistachio Loaf

<5g FIBER **4** PLANTS

The zucchini in this cake makes it really moist, and the Greek yogurt adds extra protein to moderate your blood sugar response. We've used actual brown sugar because fancy alternatives aren't really better for you. Instead, we balance your blood sugar response with the other ingredients, like nuts, yogurt, and olive oil. Enjoy!

Method

1. Preheat the oven to 350°F / 175°C and line a 2-lb / 900g loaf pan with parchment paper.

2. Grate the zucchini and place into the center of a clean kitchen towel. Wrap the grated zucchini tightly and wring out as much water as possible.

3. Put three-quarters of the pistachios into a food processor and process until as fine as possible. Transfer to a bowl with the flour, baking powder, and salt.

4. In a separate bowl, place the eggs, olive oil, yogurt, brown sugar, and lemon zest and juice and mix until smooth. Add the dry ingredients and the zucchini and fold everything together until thoroughly mixed.

5. Spoon into the prepared loaf pan. Coarsely chop the remaining pistachios and scatter on top. Bake for 50–55 minutes, or until a skewer inserted in the middle comes out clean. Allow to cool completely before removing from the pan and slicing.

Preparation time: *15 minutes*
Cook time: *1 hour*

Ingredients (Makes 10 slices)

1 medium zucchini
Scant 1 cup / 125g whole pistachios
¾ cup / 90g whole-grain spelt flour
2 tsp baking powder
Pinch of salt
3 medium eggs
¼ cup / 60ml extra-virgin olive oil
¼ cup / 60g Greek yogurt
7 tbsp packed / 85g soft light brown sugar
Zest of 1½ lemons and juice of 1

Top-ups

Yogurt to serve
Pomegranate seeds or cherries to serve

Swaps

Plant-based yogurt
Pumpkin and sunflower seeds for pistachios
Flax eggs for eggs *(see page 221)*

Chocolate–Olive Oil Mousse

5–10g FIBER **3** PLANTS

Extra-virgin olive oil and dark chocolate make for a deliciously rich and bitter combination, and a polyphenol-packed mousse. If you can, use a good-quality fruity olive oil to take this to the next level. We've used aquafaba (the liquid from a can of chickpeas) instead of egg whites; next time you use canned chickpeas in a recipe, keep the liquid and store it in the freezer for desserts like this.

Method

1. Place a heatproof bowl over a saucepan of simmering water and slowly melt the chocolate (make sure the bowl does not touch the water). When ready, remove from the heat and add the olive oil, maple syrup, and a pinch of salt. Mix to combine.

2. Put the aquafaba in the clean, grease-free bowl of a stand mixer fitted with the whisk attachment and whisk until stiff peaks form, about 8 minutes.

3. Stir a spoonful of the aquafaba into the chocolate mixture, then add the chocolate mixture to the whisked aquafaba. Use a metal spoon to gently fold the mixture together—don't beat it or you will lose the airy texture.

4. Spoon into four small glasses and refrigerate for at least 1 hour. Top with hazelnuts, cherries, an extra drizzle of olive oil, and a pinch of salt.

Preparation time: *15 minutes, plus 1 hour chilling*

Ingredients (Serves 4)

3½ oz / 100g dark chocolate
(at least 70% cocoa solids), broken into pieces

2 tbsp extra-virgin olive oil,
plus extra for drizzling

2 tsp maple syrup

1–2 pinches of salt

½ cup / 140ml aquafaba
(liquid from a can of chickpeas at room temperature)

1 cup / 150g cherries
(fresh or frozen), pitted

Top-up

Crème fraîche
Chopped hazelnuts

Swap

Honey for maple syrup

SWEET TREATS

Carrot Cake with Tahini-Orange Frosting

5–10g FIBER   **8** PLANTS

SWEET TREATS

For moments when your cup of tea needs a slice of cake, this one really packs in the plants, and the Greek yogurt "frosting" adds a lovely tartness—just be mindful it won't set like regular frosting. The added benefit of the yogurt is that the protein and fat will help slow the absorption of sugar into your bloodstream from the cake.

Method

1. Preheat the oven to 350°F / 180°C and grease and line a 9-inch / 20cm round springform cake pan with parchment paper.

2. Put the olive oil, kefir, eggs, honey, and sugar in a bowl and mix to combine. Add the almond meal, cinnamon, pumpkin seeds, walnuts, baking powder, baking soda, and salt and mix everything until thoroughly combined.

3. Fold in the carrots and then transfer the mixture to the lined pan. Flatten with a spatula and bake for 45–50 minutes, until a metal skewer inserted in the middle comes out clean. Allow to cool completely before removing from the pan.

4. Meanwhile, make the topping: mix the Greek yogurt, tahini, vanilla extract, honey, and orange zest in a bowl—it will thicken slightly. Spread all over the cooled cake and finish with the pumpkin seeds. Store in the fridge, covered, for up to 5 days.

Preparation time: *15 minutes*
Cook time: *50 minutes*

Ingredients (*Makes 8–10 slices*)

6 tbsp / 85ml extra-virgin olive oil, *plus extra for greasing*
⅓ cup / 100ml kefir
3 medium eggs
¼ cup honey
7 tbsp packed / 85g light brown sugar
2¾ cups / 285g almond meal or flour
1 tbsp ground cinnamon
¼ cup / 35g pumpkin seeds
Scant ½ cup / 50g coarsely chopped walnuts
2 tsp baking powder
1 tsp baking soda
Pinch of salt
2 large / 200g carrots, *grated*

For the topping

¾ cup / 185g Greek yogurt
2 tbsp tahini
1 tsp vanilla extract
1 tsp honey
Zest of ½ orange
2 tbsp pumpkin seeds

Top-ups

Fresh berries
Walnuts

Chia-Lemon Pots de Crème

If you top it with granola and berries, this works really well for breakfast, but it's also a delicious sweet treat. The chia seeds are high in fiber and omega-3s, and the silken tofu adds a great source of protein, making this really satisfying. You can make this vegan with plant-based milk and yogurt in place of the lemon curd, as the juice brings the lemon flavor.

Method

1. Place all the ingredients in a high-powered blender and blend until silky smooth.

2. Divide equally between glasses. Allow to rest for at least 15 minutes before serving, or chill in the fridge until needed.

<5g FIBER   **1** PLANT

Preparation time: *5 minutes*

Ingredients (Serves 2–3)

6¼ oz / 180g silken tofu
⅔ cup / 160ml milk
2 tbsp lemon curd
2 tbsp chia seeds
Juice of 1 lemon
½ tsp vanilla extract

Top-ups

Sticky Maple and Cinnamon Nut Clusters *(page 252)*
Grated dark chocolate

Swap

Plant-based yogurt or milk for lemon curd

SWEET TREATS

Mixed Berry Clafouti

5–10g FIBER   **4** PLANTS

If you have frozen berries or any other fruit on hand, this is a great recipe. The oat bran is fantastically high in fiber, and the olive oil adds polyphenols. While the kefir is baked and therefore doesn't confer a probiotic benefit, it adds fat and protein to moderate your blood sugar response. Add some live bacteria back in by pouring Greek yogurt or kefir over the top to serve.

Method

1. Preheat the oven to 400°F / 200°C and line a 9-inch / 23cm round ovenproof dish with parchment paper. Grease with a little olive oil.

2. Put the sugar, olive oil, egg, and kefir into a bowl and mix together until smooth. Stir in the oat bran, pumpkin seeds, baking powder, and salt.

3. Transfer to the lined baking dish, scatter the frozen berries all over the top, and bake for 35 minutes, until slightly risen, golden brown, and ruby red with softened berries.

Preparation time: *10 minutes*
Cook time: *25 minutes*

Ingredients (Serves 6)

⅓ cup packed / 70g light brown sugar
3 tbsp extra-virgin olive oil
1 medium egg
¾ cup plus 2 tbsp / 200ml kefir
1⅔ cups / 200g oat bran
½ cup / 70g pumpkin seeds
½ tsp baking powder
Pinch of salt
1¼ cups / 150g frozen summer / mixed berries

Top-ups

Lemon zest
Greek yogurt or extra kefir to serve
Pumpkin seeds

Swaps

Stewed rhubarb
Frozen cherries

SWEET TREATS

<5g
FIBER

3
PLANTS

Apple Pecan Strudel

Preparation time: *15 minutes*
Cook time: *20 minutes*

Ingredients (Serves 4)

2 large (or 3 medium) apples, such as Gala, *peeled and coarsely diced*
1 tsp ground cinnamon
2 tbsp honey
¾ cup / 100g pecans, *finely chopped*
2 sheets of phyllo dough
1½ tbsp extra-virgin olive oil, plus more for brushing

Top-ups

Crème fraîche
Kefir

Swap

Seeds for pecans

This is a twist on my favorite apple strudel from my time spent working in a restaurant kitchen in Austria. I've made thousands of these, but this version is much better for your blood sugar response. The olive oil adds polyphenols, and the nuts add fiber. Top with kefir for added probiotic benefits.

Method

1. Preheat the oven to 400°F / 200°C and line a baking sheet with parchment paper.

2. Put the apples into a small saucepan with 3 tablespoons of water and simmer with the lid on for 5–10 minutes, until the apples are soft but still holding their shape. Add the cinnamon and honey and stir until the liquid in the pan is glossy and coats the apples, about 5 minutes. Use a handheld blender to pulse the mixture, only partially blending it. Stir in the pecans and allow to cool slightly.

3. Lay a sheet of phyllo on a flat surface, brush all over with olive oil, then fold in half, short side to short side. Repeat with the remaining phyllo and place on top of the first layer (giving you 4 layers of phyllo).

4. Spoon the mixture in a line onto the dough 1 inch / 2.5cm from the longest edge. Shape it into a neat log. Take the edge of the phyllo closest to the apples and fold it over the mixture. Roll the phyllo up tightly to create a long log shape, tucking the ends in as you go.

5. Brush the strudel all over with the olive oil, transfer to the lined baking sheet, and bake for 20 minutes, turning halfway through. When ready, allow to cool slightly, slice, and serve.

Raspberry-Granola Crumble

10–15g FIBER   **12** PLANTS

SWEET TREATS

Next time you make the Cinnamon-Pecan Granola on page 70, double up the quantities and keep some for this delicious crumble. It will work with any mix of fruits, and you can add in other spices to mix up the flavor. Raspberries are a favorite of mine because they're so high in fiber. The compote here is also great for breakfast.

Method

1. Place the apples in a saucepan with the honey and 3 tablespoons of water. Cover with a lid and cook over low heat for 8 minutes, until the apples have softened but are still holding their shape. Stir them from time to time.

2. Add the raspberries and mix to combine. Bring to a gentle bubbling simmer and cook for 3–4 minutes.

3. Serve topped with a generous helping of granola, some yogurt, and an extra drizzle of honey if you wish!

Preparation time: *5 minutes*
Cook time: *12 minutes*

Ingredients (Serves 4)

- **3 apples,** *peeled and coarsely chopped (10 oz / 300g prepped weight)*
- **1 tbsp honey,** *plus optional extra for drizzling*
- **1 lb 5 oz / 600g fresh or frozen raspberries**
- **8 oz / 240g Cinnamon-Pecan Granola** *(page 70)*
- **6 tbsp / 100g Greek yogurt**

Top-ups

Fresh berries
Fresh mint

Swaps

Plant-based yogurt or kefir for Greek yogurt
Any mix of fresh or frozen berries

Berry "Nice" Cream

5–10g FIBER   **5** PLANTS

With a few key ingredients in your freezer, you'll always have a delicious (and polyphenol-packed) ice cream within reach. Be sure to freeze this mixture and then blend it when you're ready to eat for a deliciously smooth texture. Doing it the other way around (blending and then freezing) makes it icy and less enjoyable. Top this with nuts or granola for extra texture, fiber, and plant points.

Method

1. Place the mixed berries, banana, and nuts in a plastic tub and freeze.

2. When ready to make the ice cream, tip the frozen mixture into a food processor. Add the tofu and almond butter, then process until smooth.

3. Serve in generous scoops with a crunchy topping like chopped nuts.

Preparation time: *10 minutes, plus freezing time*

Ingredients *(Serves 2)*

1½ cups / 150g frozen mixed berries
½ banana
2½ oz / 70g nuts, *toasted and coarsely chopped*
2½ oz / 75g silken tofu
1 tbsp almond butter

Top-ups

Sticky Maple and Cinnamon Nut Clusters *(page 252)*
Cinnamon-Pecan Granola *(page 70)*

Swaps

Seed butter for nut butter
Any frozen fruit

Snacks

- 244 Recharge Bars
- 246 Beet Hummus with Seeded Crackers
- 248 Zucchini Flatbread
- 250 Chocolate Spread
- 252 Sweet and Savory Seeds and Nuts
    - Sticky Maple and Cinnamon Nut Clusters
    - Curry Cashews
- 254 Soy-Roasted Seeds
- 257 Herb and Halloumi Falafel
- 258 Dark Chocolate Bark

If you want to change one thing about the way you eat, it could pay off to change your snack habits. National surveys have shown that snacks make up around 25 percent of our energy intake, and, alarmingly, 75 percent of the calories we consume from snacks are from ultra-processed foods. As consumers, we are often fooled by so-called healthy snacks in supermarkets when, in reality, they are anything but. Simple snack swaps provide a great opportunity to improve the overall quality of the food you eat in your day.

Unlike the average snack, the recipes in this chapter are packed full of nutritious whole foods, fiber, and protein, so they will actually keep you satisfied and full until your next meal. I don't snack often, but when I do, I prefer to have a handful of nuts with a whole fruit or something that resembles a small meal to keep my energy going. If you have a stock of these delicious snacks up your sleeve, you won't be tempted to grab the first UPF item you see.

SNACKS

Recharge Bars

<5g FIBER **11** PLANTS

Give yourself a midmorning or afternoon pick-me-up with an alternative to the protein and snack bars you're likely to find in stores, which are often ultra-processed and packed with unhealthy ingredients. Bursting with plant diversity, fiber, and protein, these delicious bars are a great portable snack option. You can experiment by mixing up the flavors, nuts, and seeds to your taste, but be sure to use unsalted nuts and unsweetened cranberries here.

Method

1. Preheat the oven to 350°F / 175°C and line a deep-sided 8-inch / 20cm square baking pan with parchment paper.

2. Process the pistachios, walnuts, almonds, and coconut flakes to a fine crumb in a food processor or high-speed blender, then add to a bowl with the flaxseeds, pumpkin seeds, sunflower seeds, dried cranberries, and cinnamon and mix.

3. Put the almond butter, maple syrup, and vanilla extract in a small saucepan over low heat and stir to combine. Once it's bubbling, pour into the dry mixture and mix so that all the dry ingredients are thoroughly coated.

4. Transfer to the prepared baking pan, then press down firmly so that it spreads into each corner and is tightly packed into the pan. Bake for 30 minutes, until golden and firm. When ready, allow to cool completely in the pan.

5. Melt the chocolate in a double boiler or a heatproof bowl set over a saucepan of barely simmering water (make sure the bottom of the bowl doesn't touch the water). Drizzle the melted chocolate all over the baked nuts and seeds and let sit at room temperature until set. When the chocolate is hard, use a sharp knife to slice into 12 bars. Store in an airtight container for up to 1 week.

Preparation time: *15 minutes*
Cook time: *30–35 minutes*

Ingredients *(Makes 12 bars)*

⅓ cup / 50g pistachios
½ cup / 50g walnuts
Scant ½ cup / 50g slivered almonds
½ cup / 20g unsweetened coconut flakes
Scant ½ cup / 75g flaxseeds
¾ cup / 100g pumpkin seeds
½ cup / 70g sunflower seeds
⅓ cup / 50g dried cranberries
1½ tsp ground cinnamon
5 tbsp almond butter
7 tbsp maple syrup
1 tsp vanilla extract
2¾ oz / 80g dark chocolate (at least 70% cocoa solids)

Swap

Seed butter or any other nut butter for almond butter

Beet Hummus with Seeded Crackers

10–15g FIBER   **8** PLANTS

I love the vibrant color of the beets here, which help lower blood pressure. Treat this hummus as a base recipe and flavor it with other ingredients such as herbs, roasted red peppers, or harissa. You can add different spices and seeds to the crackers, making them a delicious portable snack. The flaxseed meal binds them and carries phytoestrogens that benefit your gut health.

Method

1. Preheat the oven to 300°F / 150°C. Put all the ingredients for the seeded crackers into a bowl and add ¾ cup / 170ml of water. Mix together and set aside for 15 minutes to thicken.

2. Spread the mixture out onto a large sheet of parchment paper (the same size as your baking sheet) and place another parchment sheet the same size on top. Use a rolling pin to roll it out as thin as possible, then transfer to the baking sheet. Peel off the top layer of parchment and bake the mixture for 1 hour, or until dry in the center.

3. Meanwhile, put the chickpeas, beet, tahini, lemon juice, and garlic in a blender with a few ice cubes. Blend until smooth, adding a few tablespoons of water if necessary to thin out the mixture. Taste and adjust the seasoning.

4. When the crackers are ready, allow them to cool completely, then break into pieces. They will keep for a week in an airtight container. Serve with the hummus.

Preparation time: *25 minutes*
Cook time: *1 hour*

Ingredients (Serves 4, with crackers left over)

For the seeded crackers

¾ cup / 80g flaxseed meal
3 tbsp chia seeds
3½ oz / 100g any mixed seeds
Pinch of salt

For the hummus

1 (14-oz / 400g) can chickpeas, *drained*
1 precooked beet *(use vacuum-packed for ease)*
2 tbsp tahini
Juice of 1 lemon
1 garlic clove
Ice cubes
Salt and black pepper

Top-ups

Sauerkraut Dressing (page 271) as an extra dip
Caraway or nigella seeds for the crackers

Swaps

Any roasted root vegetables for beet
Mixed herbs for beet

Zucchini Flatbread

We've created a hybrid between two of our most popular ZOE Instagram recipes based on Italian favorites: farinata and zucchini scarpaccia. The chickpea flour is a great alternative to wheat flour, adding protein and fiber, and the zucchini and red onion become deliciously caramelized in the batter. This could be fantastic at breakfast or as an alternative to flatbread. It's great served with the Beet Hummus or with kimchi.

Method

1. Use the slicer attachment on a food processor to very thinly slice the zucchini and onion (this can also be done by hand). Transfer to a wide bowl and scatter over the salt, massaging it into the vegetables until they begin to release their juices, about 20 minutes. Lay a small plate on top and weight it down with something heavy to help extract excess liquid.

2. Preheat the oven to 400°F / 200°C and line a rimmed 9 x 13-inch / 23 x 33cm baking dish with parchment paper. Drain the zucchini, discarding the excess liquid. Add the chickpea flour to the drained zucchini and onion and mix to create a batter. Add the lemon zest, chile flakes, a generous pinch of pepper, and 1 tablespoon of the olive oil. Mix again.

3. Drizzle ½ tablespoon of olive oil onto the parchment paper, then spread the mixture onto the dish. Scatter the rosemary (if using) over the top and drizzle with the remaining tablespoon of olive oil. Bake for 50 minutes, until the flatbread is golden and crispy at the edges. Allow to cool before slicing. The flatbread will keep for a few days in the fridge.

<5g FIBER

6 PLANTS

Preparation time: *20 minutes*
Cook time: *50 minutes*

Ingredients (Serves 8)

3 medium zucchini
 (about 1¾ lb / 750g)
1 red onion, *halved*
1 tsp sea salt
1¼ cups / 150g chickpea flour
Zest of ½ lemon
1 tsp chile flakes
2½ tbsp extra-virgin olive oil
1–2 sprigs of rosemary,
 leaves picked (optional)
Black pepper

Top-ups

Beet Hummus (*page 246*)
Kimchi

Swap

Thyme leaves for rosemary

Chocolate Spread

<5g FIBER **3** PLANTS

Making this nutty chocolate spread is incredibly easy, and even without the usual palm oils and unwanted additives, it will last in the fridge for a full 2 weeks. Use it as a dip for Seeded Crackers (page 246) and fruits such as apples, or spread it on sourdough or seeded bread. This will be popular with any children in your life, so get ready to share.

Preparation time: *10 minutes*
Cook time: *8 minutes*

Ingredients *(Makes 12 oz / 350g)*

1 cup / 140g blanched hazelnuts
1 cup / 150g sunflower seeds
3½ oz / 100g dark chocolate
 (at least 70% cocoa solids)
1 tbsp maple syrup or honey

Swap

Blanched almonds for hazelnuts

Method

1. Preheat the oven to 350°F / 180°C and line a baking sheet with parchment paper.

2. Lay the hazelnuts and sunflower seeds on the lined sheet in a single layer and toast in the oven for 8–10 minutes. Check continuously, as oven temperatures vary and nuts burn quickly. You want the nuts and seeds to be golden.

3. Put the chocolate in a heatproof bowl set over a saucepan of barely simmering water, making sure the bowl does not touch the water. Stir until melted.

4. When the nuts are ready, transfer to a food processor or high-powered blender and blend continuously for 6–8 minutes (scraping down the sides when necessary), until smooth—the mixture will resemble nut butter.

5. Add the melted chocolate and maple syrup and blend once more to combine. Transfer to a jar, refrigerate, and use within 2 weeks.

Sweet and Savory Seeds and Nuts

Some people gravitate toward sweet snacks, while others prefer savory. These recipes cover all the bases. Because they travel well, you'll never be without a satisfying snack when hunger strikes.

Sticky Maple and Cinnamon Nut Clusters

<5g FIBER **3** PLANTS

When you feel like having a sweet snack, reach for these maple syrup and cinnamon nut treats. The protein and fiber help slow your blood sugar response to the maple syrup (or honey, if you prefer), and the cinnamon brings your plant score up to three. With these in your bag, you'll always have the perfect snack on hand.

Method

1. Preheat the oven to 350°F / 180°C and line a baking sheet with parchment paper.

2. Coarsely chop the pecans and walnuts and add to a bowl with the cinnamon and salt. Toss to coat, then add the maple syrup. Use a spoon or spatula to mix the syrup and nuts together so they are thoroughly coated.

3. Spread out on the lined sheet in a single layer and roast in the oven for 7–10 minutes, until the mixture is golden and the syrup is bubbling slightly. When ready, allow to cool completely and then break into clusters. Store in an airtight container for up to 1 week.

Preparation time: *5 minutes*
Cook time: *10 minutes*

Ingredients *(Serves 6 as a snack)*

1 cup / 100g pecans
1 cup / 100g walnuts
1 tsp ground cinnamon
¼ tsp sea salt
2½ tbsp maple syrup or honey

Swaps

Almonds, hazelnuts, or cashews

Photograph on page 255

<5g
FIBER

5
PLANTS

Curry Cashews

Preparation time: *5 minutes*
Cook time: *8–10 minutes*

Ingredients *(Serves 4 as a snack)*

1 tbsp dried curry leaves
   (optional)
2 tsp curry powder
½ tsp chile powder
   (or more if you like spice)
Pinch of salt
1 tsp extra-virgin olive oil
1½ cups / 200g cashews

Top-up

Add a selection of nuts

Photograph on page 255

Including curry spices in food has been shown to improve gut microbiome composition, so these cashews are fantastic gems of goodness in their own right. Having nuts as a snack before a meal provides a good source of fiber and healthy fats, helping with your blood sugar response to the meal you eat directly after.

Method

1. Preheat the oven to 400°F / 200°C and line a baking sheet with parchment paper.

2. If using, put the curry leaves into a blender or spice grinder with the spices and salt. Blend until very finely chopped. Transfer to a bowl and mix with the olive oil, then toss with the cashews.

3. Spread out on the lined baking sheet and roast in the oven for 8 minutes, stirring halfway through. When ready, allow to cool and store in an airtight container.

Soy-Roasted Seeds

<5g
FIBER

3
PLANTS

You can enjoy these seeds on their own, so it's worth keeping them in a little plastic container to have with you for a healthy on-the-go snack. They're also delicious on top of salads or other dishes to add even more fiber—a bit of nori seaweed is a great snack for your gut microbes, for example.

Preparation time: *5 minutes*
Cook time: *5–7 minutes*

Ingredients (Serves 8 as a snack)

¾ cup / 100g pumpkin seeds
⅔ cup / 100g sunflower seeds
1½ tbsp soy sauce
1 sheet of nori *(optional)*

Top-up

Add more seeds

Photograph on page 255

Method

1. Preheat the oven to 400°F / 200°C and line a baking sheet with parchment paper.

2. Mix the seeds and soy sauce together and spread out on the lined sheet. Roast in the oven for 5–7 minutes, until golden and crisp.

3. If using, tear up the sheet of nori and put into a blender. Process into small flakes, the size of your seeds. Transfer the seeds and nori flakes to an airtight jar, shake to mix, and store until needed.

<5g
FIBER

7
PLANTS

Herb and Halloumi Falafel

Preparation time: *15 minutes*
Cook time: *30 minutes*

Ingredients (Makes 12 falafels)

1 (14-oz / 400g) can chickpeas, *drained*
1¾ oz / 50g mix of herbs *(mint, parsley, basil, chives, cilantro)*
2¾ oz / 80g halloumi, *coarsely grated*
2½ tbsp extra-virgin olive oil
1 tbsp tahini
2 tsp harissa
1 tbsp chickpea flour
Salt and black pepper

Top-ups

Greek yogurt
Hummus

Swaps

Any white beans for chickpeas
Vegan cheese for halloumi

Make this versatile recipe ahead of time and add it to sandwiches or salads or have it as a snack with hummus. Grated halloumi adds fantastic texture and flavor, and using canned chickpeas that are dried in the oven means you get a similar result to dried chickpeas (which need overnight soaking), but in a lot less time. You can freeze these before or after cooking.

Method

1. Preheat the oven to 400°F / 200°C and line a baking sheet with parchment paper. Spread the drained chickpeas onto the baking sheet and place in the oven for 10 minutes, until they have dried out.

2. Place the herbs in a food processor and blend until finely chopped. Add the halloumi, 2 tablespoons of the olive oil, the tahini, harissa, chickpea flour, and a generous pinch of salt and pepper. Add the toasted chickpeas when they are ready and blend until the mixture clumps together.

3. Using your hands, shape into 12 neat falafels. Brush each one with the remaining olive oil and bake in the oven for 20 minutes, or until golden and crisp.

4. Serve immediately with hummus or Greek yogurt, or store in the fridge for up to 3–4 days.

Dark Chocolate Bark

<5g FIBER **6** PLANTS

The seeds, nuts, and chocolate work in tandem to make this a surprisingly healthy yet decadent snack. Add any selection of nuts and seeds you like, so long as it totals around 5¼ oz / 150g. Once cooled, you can store this in the fridge for up to 2 weeks.

Method

1. Break the chocolate into pieces and put into a heatproof bowl set over a saucepan of barely simmering water (making sure the bowl does not touch the water). Stir until melted. Coarsely chop the nuts and seeds.

2. Line a baking sheet with parchment paper and spread the melted chocolate out in a thin, even layer. Scatter the seeds and nuts all over the top and use a spoon or knife to gently swirl them into the chocolate—they don't need to be fully covered, just embedded in the chocolate enough so they don't fall off when it sets.

3. Scatter the sea salt all over the chocolate bark and leave for at least 2 hours to cool and set. When ready, break into small (2-inch / 5cm) shards and store in an airtight container in the fridge, or a cool place. The bark will keep for 2 weeks.

Preparation time: *10 minutes, plus 2 hours cooling time*

Ingredients *(Makes 15 servings)*

5¼ oz / 150g dark chocolate *(at least 70% cocoa solids)*
¼ cup / 30g pistachios
¼ cup / 30g pecans
¼ cup / 30g almonds
¼ cup / 30g pumpkin seeds
Scant ¼ cup / 30g sunflower seeds
¼ tsp sea salt

Top-up

Dried cranberries

Swap

Any seeds for nuts

Score Boosters

262 Nut Crumb

265 Seed Mix Sprinkle

266 Booster Bouillon

269 Mixed ACV Pickles

270 Four Fermented Salad Dressings

 Miso Dressing

 Kimchi Dressing

 Kefir Dressing

 Sauerkraut Dressing

My food philosophy is that we should be adding more to our plate, not taking things away. This abundance mindset is what makes eating over 30 different plants each week possible, and so I love this chapter because it will help you bring diversity to your meal with minimal effort. There are lots of ferments in here that appear in surprising ways. For example, the four delicious dressings each include a unique ferment that adds a gut-friendly boost to your salads. Lots of versatile score boosters find their way into recipes throughout the book, but they can also make great snacks in their own right. Having them in the fridge or in a jar makes it easy to add a sprinkle here and there, plus it has the added benefit (or not) of making your fridge look like a science experiment, just like mine.

Nut Crumb

<5g FIBER **4** PLANTS

Most dishes would benefit from a sprinkle of nut crumb, as its flavors marry beautifully; plus it brings four extra plants to any recipe. It will keep for 4 weeks in an airtight jar, and you can try experimenting with different herbs, nuts, and seeds to add different flavors. Try it on top of soups, salads, pastas, or any recipe that could use contrasting texture and flavor.

Method

1. Preheat the oven to 350°F / 180°C. Put the nuts and herbs onto a nonstick baking sheet and season with the salt and pepper.

2. Place in the oven for 8–10 minutes, until the nuts are turning golden and the herbs look dried and crisp. Keep a very close eye, as the nuts burn quickly.

3. Allow the nuts to cool completely, then transfer to a food processor and process until they resemble chunky breadcrumbs. Stored in an airtight jar, these will keep for 4 weeks.

Preparation time: *10 minutes*
Cook time: *8–10 minutes*

Ingredients *(Makes 9 oz / 250g)*

1¼ cups / 150g whole hazelnuts
1 cup / 150g whole almonds
1 oz / 25g fresh thyme,
    leaves picked
1 oz / 25g fresh rosemary,
    leaves picked
1 tsp sea salt
Generous pinch of black pepper

Swap

Any other nuts for hazelnuts and almonds

Photograph on page 165

SCORE BOOSTERS

<5g
FIBER

5
PLANTS

Seed Mix Sprinkle

Preparation time: *5 minutes*

Ingredients *(Makes about 3⅔ cups / 550g)*

⅔ cup / 100g golden flaxseeds
¾ cup / 100g sesame seeds
1 cup / 150g sunflower seeds
1 cup / 150g pumpkin seeds
¼ cup / 50g chia seeds

Swap

Use any combination of seeds

Photograph on page 97

This seed mix appears throughout the chapters, featuring in recipes such as Miso-Spinach Eggs, Zucchini Lima Beans with Tomato Salsa, or Raspberry-Lemon Pancakes (pages 94, 171, and 81). It's versatile, increasing the plant score and adding texture in both sweet and savory recipes alike. I change mine every week by topping up my jar using new and interesting seeds, and it's become a real staple in my life.

Method

Mix all the ingredients together and transfer to a jar. The mixture will last for months if kept in a cool, dry part of your kitchen.

Boosting Bouillon

<5g FIBER   **2** PLANTS

This is a fantastic ZOE alternative to using stock cubes, imparting a deep umami flavor, which is why you'll see it featured in so many of the recipes in this book. The chile flakes add a gentle warmth to the overall taste, but you can exclude them if you wish. Use 2–3 tablespoons to replace 1 stock cube. You can feel good knowing that, each time you use it, you're boosting your plant score and fiber intake.

Method

Place all the ingredients in a blender and blend until you have a fine powder. Store in an airtight jar for up to 4 weeks.

Preparation time: *5 minutes*

Ingredients *(Makes about 5¼ oz / 150g)*

½ cup plus 2 tbsp / 50g nutritional yeast
½ cup / 70g sunflower seeds
2 tbsp sea salt
1 tbsp chile flakes

Photograph on page 101

SCORE BOOSTERS

5–10g
FIBER

2
PLANTS

Pearls and Puy

Preparation time: *3 minutes*
Cook time: *35 minutes*

Ingredients *(Serves 2–4)*

½ **cup / 100g green (Puy) lentils**
½ **cup / 100g pearl barley**
Salt

Photograph on page 39

Rice is the most commonly eaten grain in the world, but it isn't the most nutritious and doesn't give your gut microbiome the fiber it desires. Mixing up your grains is a great way to help you reach your 30 plants a week. This combination provides plenty of plant protein and fiber, so it's great for moderating your blood sugar response.

Method

1. Place the lentils and barley in a medium saucepan and cover with 4 cups / 1L of water. Bring to a boil, then reduce the heat and simmer, covered with a lid, for 35 minutes, until the lentils and barley are tender and the water has been absorbed.

2. Drain, season with a pinch of salt, and serve as an alternative to rice.

Tempeh Crumble

<5g
FIBER

2
PLANTS

If you're new to tempeh, this is the ideal recipe for you. Tempeh comes from Indonesia, and is made from fermented soybeans. It's packed with protein and fiber, so adding this crispy crumble to dishes is not only satisfying but also helps reduce your blood sugar response. The smaller you make the pieces, the crisper they will become. Add to dishes for an umami flavor or pack it in a lidded plastic container for a portable plant-based snack.

Preparation time: *8 minutes*
Cook time: *20 minutes*

Ingredients (Serves 4, as a top-up)

1 tsp soy sauce
1 tsp miso
1 (7-oz / 200g) block of tempeh
Black pepper

Swap

Gochujang for miso

Method

1. Preheat the oven to 400°F / 200°C and line a baking sheet with parchment paper. Mix the soy sauce and miso in a medium bowl until smooth.

2. Crumble the tempeh into very small pieces and toss with the soy sauce and miso. Season with pepper, spread out onto the lined sheet, and bake for 15–20 minutes, until golden and crisp. Keep refrigerated for up to 3 days.

Crispy Pulses and Grains

Introduce pulses and grains to more of your meals by baking them in the oven until crisp. They're like a blank canvas, and you can use either sweet or savory flavors.

<5g **4**
FIBER PLANTS

Preparation time: *5 minutes*
Cook time: *15–20 minutes*

Ingredients (Serves 4, as a top-up)

½ recipe Pearls and Puy
 (page 265), patted dry
2 tsp extra-virgin olive oil
½ tsp honey or maple syrup
½ tsp ground cinnamon
1 tbsp unsweetened nut butter

Sweet Crispy Pulses and Grains

These are great with Tim's Break-fast Bowl or the Spiced Pear Oatmeal (pages 76 and 92).

Method

1. Preheat the oven to 400°F / 200°C.

2. Toss the Pearls and Puy with the olive oil, honey, cinnamon, and nut butter. Spread out on a nonstick baking sheet and bake in the oven for 15–20 minutes, until crisp (stir after the first 10 minutes if necessary). Leave to cool before storing in an airtight container for up to 3 days.

<5g **3**
FIBER PLANTS

Preparation time: *5 minutes*
Cook time: *15–20 minutes*

Ingredients (Serves 2, as a top-up)

½ recipe Pearls and Puy
 (page 265), patted dry
1 tbsp extra-virgin olive oil
½ tsp chile powder or paprika
Salt and black pepper

Savory Crispy Pulses and Grains

These are great with salads, as well as dishes like Palak Tofu or Mushroom Stroganoff with Lima Bean Mash (pages 169 and 157).

Method

1. Preheat the oven to 400°F / 200°C.

2. Toss the Pearls and Puy with the olive oil and chile powder and season. Spread out on a nonstick baking sheet and bake in the oven for 15–20 minutes, until crisp (stir after the first 10 minutes if necessary). Leave to cool before storing in an airtight container for up to 3 days.

Cashew Cream

<5g
FIBER

1
PLANT

If you eat a plant-based diet, this is a fantastic replacement for yogurt and works well in many of the recipes in the Mornings chapter. You can add it to curries alongside coconut milk to increase the plant score, and with a little vanilla extract mixed in, it makes a great alternative to cream in the Sweet Treats chapter. If you have a high-powered blender, you won't even need to wait for the nuts to soak.

Method

1. Soak the cashews in ¾ cup plus 2 tablespoons / 200ml of water for 30 minutes.

2. Transfer the cashews and their water to a blender with the lemon juice and blend until smooth. Store in the fridge for up to 1 week. The cream may thicken slightly when cold—simply thin it out with a little water if necessary.

Preparation time: *35 minutes*

Ingredients *(Makes 1 cup / 250ml)*

1 cup / 130g cashews
Juice of 1 lemon

Top-up

1 tsp vanilla extract (for sweet cream)

SCORE BOOSTERS

<5g FIBER   **3** PLANTS

Mixed ACV Pickles

Preparation time: *15 minutes*

Ingredients *(Makes one 1-qt / 1L jar)*

1 large fennel bulb
1 red onion
4 celery stalks
1¼ cups / 300ml live/raw apple cider vinegar
2 tbsp sugar
½ tbsp sea salt

Swap

Any 18-oz / 500g mix of vegetables for the fennel, onion, and celery

Photograph on page 65

I generally prefer ferments to pickles, but this version uses live, or raw, apple cider vinegar (ACV), resulting in a pickle with probiotic benefits, great acidity, and crunch. By this stage you'll know to add any veggies you might have. I sometimes like to give simple red onions a quick pickle to add flavor (and a vibrant pink color) to dishes like the Corn Fritters (page 96). You'll need a 1½-pint / 500ml glass or ceramic preserving jar, but there's no need to sterilize; just make sure you clean well by hand or, ideally, in a dishwasher. These pickles will last up to a month in the fridge—add them liberally to almost anything!

Method

1. Wash the jar in soapy water and rinse clean. Place the slicer attachment on a food processor and finely slice the vegetables, or slice thinly by hand, using a mandoline if you have one.

2. Tightly pack the sliced vegetables into the jar. Mix the apple cider vinegar with ⅓ cup / 80ml of water and the sugar and salt. Pour into the jar and press the vegetables down until fully submerged, then seal with the lid.

3. The pickles will be ready to use almost immediately, but the flavor will become more pronounced over time. It will keep in the fridge for up to 1 month.

Four Fermented Salad Dressings

SCORE BOOSTERS

Made with four of my favorite ferments—miso, kimchi, kefir, and sauerkraut—these dressings bring the added benefit of an instant plant and probiotic boost to any dish. We've signposted recipes you can add them to, but don't be shy about adorning any meal with them. In this case, more is more for your gut microbes.

Miso Dressing

<5g FIBER **3** PLANTS **Prep time:** 5 minutes

Ingredients (Makes ¾ cup / 170ml)

3 tbsp tahini
3 tbsp apple cider vinegar
1 tbsp miso
1 (1-inch / 2.5cm) piece of ginger, finely grated
Black pepper

This dressing is great with the Eggplant Noodle Salad (page 132) and would make a fantastic alternative dressing for the Kale and Mushroom Salad (page 149).

Method

1. Put the first 4 ingredients in a bowl with 3 tablespoons of cold water and mix vigorously. Add a few more tablespoons of water if necessary to reach a consistency similar to half-and-half.

2. Season with a pinch of pepper and store in an airtight container in the fridge for up to 2 weeks.

Kimchi Dressing

<5g FIBER **4** PLANTS **Prep time:** 5 minutes

Ingredients (Makes ⅞ cup / 200ml)

2 oz / 60g silken tofu
3 tbsp kimchi *(including brine)*
2 tbsp miso
2 tbsp apple cider vinegar
4 tbsp extra-virgin olive oil
Pinch of salt

Full of umami and spicy flavor, this is fantastic with the Polyphenol Salad (page 141), as a condiment alongside the Eggplant Schnitzel (page 164), or as a replacement for mayo in a wrap.

Method

Place all the ingredients in a blender and blend until smooth. Store in an airtight container in the fridge for up to 2 weeks.

Kefir Dressing

<5g FIBER   **4** PLANTS   **Prep time:** 8 minutes

Ingredients (Makes 1 cup / 250ml)

1 small ripe avocado *(3 oz / 90g prepped weight)*
1¾ oz / 20g cilantro
Zest and juice of 2 limes
2 tbsp apple cider vinegar
½ cup / 125ml kefir
2 pickled green chiles, *plus 2 tbsp brine*
Pinch of salt

Swap

Cashew Cream *(page 268)* **for kefir**

Great on the Greens and Beans Salad (page 134) and the Carrot and Fennel Salad with Halloumi (page 142). It's also delicious spooned onto Corn Fritters (page 96).

Method

Put all the ingredients into a blender and blend until smooth. Store in an airtight container in the fridge for up to 1 week.

Sauerkraut Dressing

<5g FIBER   **4** PLANTS   **Prep time:** 5 minutes

Ingredients (Makes ⅞ cup / 200ml)

1 oz / 30g basil
2 roasted red peppers from a jar *(4 oz / 120g)*
3 tbsp Sauerkraut, *(page 64), plus 3 tbsp brine (1¼ oz / 35g)*
2 tbsp extra-virgin olive oil
Salt and black pepper

Along with its probiotics, the sauerkraut adds a unique flavor to this dressing. Delicious with salads, it's also a great dip for crudités or the Seeded Crackers on page 246. It keeps well in the fridge for up to 1 week.

Method

Put all the ingredients into a blender with a pinch of salt and pepper and blend until smooth. The dressing will keep in an airtight container in the fridge for up to 1 week. Thin with a little water if necessary.

Index

Recipe index

11-Plant Orzo, 163

aioli, 216
almonds
    Dark Chocolate Bark, 258
    Nut Crumb, 262
    Recharge Bars, 244
Always-There Risotto, 178
Anchovy and Artichoke Pasta, 195
apples
    Apple Pecan Strudel, 237
    Probiotic Bircher Muesli, 88
    Raspberry-Granola Crumble, 238
artichokes
    Anchovy and Artichoke Pasta, 195
    Artichoke and Sun-Dried Tomato Stew, 191
    Artichoke Lima Beans, 109
    Lima Bean Caesar, 126
    Prebiotic Greek Salad, 145
    Sheet-Pan Artichoke and Olive Bake, 160
Arugula
    Lima Bean Caesar, 126
    Greens and Beans Salad, 134
    Prebiotic Greek Salad, 145
Asparagus–Pearl Barley Risotto, 166
avocado
    Black Bean Avocado Toast, 84
    Green Goddess Chickpea Sandwich, 110
    Greens and Beans Salad, 134
    Kefir Dressing, 271
    Pomegranate-Lentil Salad, 129
    Tricolore Seeded Bruschetta, 122

beans
    11-Plant Orzo, 163
    Artichoke and Sun-Dried Tomato Stew, 191
    Artichoke Lima Beans, 109
    Beans Three Ways, 106–9
    Black Bean Avocado Toast, 84
    Black Bean Chili, 210
    Black Bean "Meat" Balls, 180
    Braised Beans and Greens, 196
    Bulgur Wheat with Aioli, 216
    Cashew-Cream Green Curry, 154
    Creamy Kale Pasta, 100
    Green Shakshuka, 82
    Greens and Beans Salad, 134
    Juno's Lasagna, 203
    Kale and Mushroom Salad, 149
    Lima Bean Caesar, 126
    Minestrone, 188
    Mushroom Stroganoff with Lima Bean Mash, 157
    Roasted Squash with Toasted Grains, 204
    Sheet-Pan Artichoke and Olive Bake, 160
    Spicy Gochujang Beans, 87
    Tahini-Miso Beans, 106
    Whole Roast Cauliflower, 215
    Zucchini Butter Beans with Tomato Salsa, 171
beets
    Beety Brownies, 222
    Beet Hummus with Seeded Crackers, 246
berries
    Berry "Nice" Cream, 240
    Mixed Berry Clafouti, 234
    Raspberry-Granola Crumble, 238
    Raspberry-Lemon Pancakes, 81
    Tim's Break-fast Bowl, 76
Bircher Muesli, Probiotic, 88
black beans
    Black Bean Avocado Toast, 84
    Black Bean Chili, 210
    Black Bean "Meat" Balls, 180
    Cashew-Cream Green Curry, 154
    Greens and Beans Salad, 134
Boosting Bouillon, 264
Bouillon, Boosting, 264
Braised Beans and Greens, 196
bread
    Black Bean Avocado Toast, 84
    Green Goddess Chickpea Sandwich, 110
    Harissa Mushrooms Seeded Bruschetta, 120
    Kimchi Broccoli Seeded Bruschetta, 123
    Miso-Spinach Eggs, 94
    Nut-and-Seed Loaf, 73
    Seeded Soda Bread, 68
    Spinach Wraps with Roasted Pepper, 114
    Tricolore Seeded Bruschetta, 122
    Zucchini Flatbread, 248
broccoli
    Broccolini and Walnut Orecchiette, 174
    Bulgur with Aioli, 216
    Cashew-Cream Green Curry, 154
    Kimchi Broccoli Seeded Bruschetta, 123
    Roasted Broccolini–Tahini Salad, 130
    Smashed Pea Bowl, 103
    Zucchini Lima Beans with Tomato Salsa, 171

Brownies, Beety, 222
bruschetta
    Harissa Mushrooms Seeded, 120
    Kimchi Broccoli Seeded, 123
    Tricolore Seeded, 122
bulgur wheat
    Bulgur Bowl, 146
    Bulgur with Aioli, 216
    Pomegranate Tabbouleh, 138
butternut squash *see* **squash**

cabbage
    Kefir Curried Chickpeas, 119
    Polyphenol Salad, 141
    Sauerkraut, 64
    Sauerkraut Frittata, 91
    Sheet-Pan Harissa Cabbage, 172
    Simple Kimchi, 67
Cacio e Pepe Chickpeas, 108
cakes
    Beety Brownies, 222
    Carrot Cake with Tahini Orange Frosting, 230
    Lemon Pistachio Loaf, 224
cannellini beans
    Braised Beans and Greens, 196
    Creamy Kale Pasta, 100
    Juno's Lasagna, 203
    Minestrone, 188
    Roasted Squash with Toasted Grains, 204
    Tahini-Miso Beans, 106
capers: Pea Soup with Crispy Caper Chickpeas, 184
carrots
    Artichoke and Sun-Dried Tomato Stew, 191
    Black Bean "Meat" Balls, 180
    Carrot and Fennel Salad with Halloumi, 142
    Carrot Cake with Tahini Orange Frosting, 230
    Harissa-Hazelnut Roast, 212
    Instant Noodles, 116
    Juno's Lasagna, 203
    Minestrone, 188
    Polyphenol Salad, 141
cashews
    Cashew-Cream Green Curry, 154
    Cashew Cream, 268
    Coconut Spinach Lentils, 192
    Curry Cashews, 253
    Kale and Cashew Soup, 113

    Lima Bean Caesar, 126
    Palak Tofu, 169
cauliflower
    Polyphenol Salad, 141
    Whole Roast Cauliflower, 215
celery
    Black Bean "Meat" Balls, 180
    Harissa-Hazelnut Roast, 212
    Juno's Lasagna, 203
    Minestrone, 188
    Mixed ACV Pickles, 269
    Pea Soup with Crispy Caper Chickpeas, 184
cheddar
    Juno's Lasagna, 203
    Mushroom and Leek Tart, 209
chestnuts: Mushroom Stroganoff with Lima Bean Mash, 157
Chia-Lemon Pots de Crème, 232
chickpeas
    Anchovy and Artichoke Pasta, 195
    Beet Hummus with Seeded Crackers, 246
    Cacio e Pepe Chickpeas, 108
    Green Goddess Chickpea Sandwich, 110
    Herb and Halloumi Falafel, 257
    Kefir Curried Chickpeas, 119
    Pea Soup with Crispy Caper Chickpeas, 184
    Roasted Broccolini–Tahini Salad, 130
    Sheet-Pan Harissa Cabbage, 172
    Sheet-Pan Roasted Eggplant, 200
Chili, Black Bean, 210
chocolate
    Beety Brownies, 222
    Chocolate–Olive Oil Mousse, 226
    Chocolate Spread, 250
    Dark Chocolate Bark, 258
    Pecan Chocolate Cookies, 221
    Recharge Bars, 244
Cinnamon-Pecan Granola, 70
Clafouti, Mixed Berry, 234
coconut
    Cashew-Cream Green Curry, 154
    Cinnamon-Pecan Granola, 70
    Coconut Spinach Lentils, 192
    Recharge Bars, 244
Cookies, Pecan Chocolate, 221
corn
    Corn Fritters, 96
    Corn and Spinach Dal, 187
    Hazelnut Gremolata–Corn Salad, 104

cottage cheese
    Herby Green-Pea Pancakes, 78
    Raspberry-Lemon Pancakes, 81
Crackers, Seeded, 246
cranberries: Recharge Bars, 244
cranberry beans
    Artichoke and Sun-Dried Tomato Stew, 191
    Green Shakshuka, 82
    Sheet-Pan Artichoke and Olive Bake, 160
Creamy Kale Pasta, 100
crispy pulses and grains
    Savory, 267
    Sweet, 267
Crumble, Raspberry Granola, 238
Crumble, Tempeh, 266
cucumber
    Pomegranate Tabbouleh, 138
    Prebiotic Greek Salad, 145
curry
    Cashew-Cream Green Curry, 154
    Coconut Spinach Lentils, 192
    Curry Cashews, 253
    Diversity Dal, 158
    Kefir Curried Chickpeas, 119
    Palak Tofu, 169
    Corn and Spinach Dal, 187

dal
    Corn and Spinach Dal, 187
    Diversity Dal, 158
Dal, Diversity, 158
Dark Chocolate Bark, 258
Diversity Dal, 158
dressings, 125
    Kefir, 271
    Kimchi, 270
    Miso, 270
    Sauerkraut, 271

Edam: Eggplant Schnitzel, 164
Eggplant
    Bulgur Bowl, 146
    Eggplant Noodle Salad, 132
    Eggplant Parmigiana, 152
    Eggplant Schnitzel, 164
    Sheet-Pan Harissa Cabbage, 172
    Sheet-Pan Roasted Eggplant, 200
eggs
    Green Shakshuka, 82
    Herby Green-Pea Pancakes, 78
    Miso-Spinach Eggs, 94
    Sauerkraut Frittata, 91

Falafel, Herb and Halloumi, 257
fennel
    Carrot and Fennel Salad with Halloumi, 142
    Mixed ACV Pickles, 265
feta cheese
    Prebiotic Greek Salad, 145
    Sheet-Pan Artichoke and Olive Bake, 160
    Spinach Wraps with Roasted Pepper, 114
Flatbread, Zucchini, 248
Frittata, Sauerkraut, 91
Fritters, Corn, 96

granola
    Cinnamon-Pecan Granola, 70
    Raspberry-Granola Crumble, 238
grapefruit: Greens and Beans Salad, 134
green beans
    Artichoke and Sun-Dried Tomato Stew, 191
    Bulgur with Aioli, 216
    Cashew-Cream Green Curry, 154
Green Goddess Chickpea Sandwich, 110
Green Shakshuka, 82
Greens and Beans Salad, 134

halloumi
    Carrot and Fennel Salad with Halloumi, 142
    Corn Fritters, 96
    Herb and Halloumi Falafel, 257
    Sheet-Pan Roasted Eggplant, 200
harissa
    Harissa-Hazelnut Roast, 212
    Harissa Mushrooms Seeded Bruschetta, 120
    Sheet-Pan Harissa Cabbage, 172
hazelnuts
    Chocolate Spread, 250
    Harissa-Hazelnut Roast, 212
    Hazelnut Gremolata–Corn Salad, 104
    Nut Crumb, 262
    Prebiotic Greek Salad, 145
    Red Pepper–Quinoa Salad, 136
Herb and Halloumi Falafel, 257
Herby Green-Pea Pancakes, 78
Hummus, Beet, with Seeded Crackers, 246

ice cream: Berry "Nice" Cream, 240
Instant Noodles, 116

Juno's Lasagna, 203

kale
   Creamy Kale Pasta, 100
   Green Shakshuka, 82
   Kale and Cashew Soup, 113
   Kale and Mushroom Salad, 149

kefir
   Carrot and Fennel Salad with Halloumi, 142
   Green Goddess Chickpea Sandwich, 110
   Kefir Curried Chickpeas, 119
   Kefir Dressing, 271
   Mushroom Stroganoff with Lima Bean Mash, 157
   Probiotic Bircher Muesli, 88
   Tim's Break-fast Bowl, 76

kimchi
   Instant Noodles, 116
   Kale and Cashew Soup, 113
   Kimchi Broccoli Seeded Bruschetta, 123
   Kimchi Dressing, 270
   Simple Kimchi, 67
   Tahini-Miso Beans, 106

Lasagna, Juno's, 203

leeks
   11-Plant Orzo, 163
   Asparagus–Pearl Barley Risotto, 166
   Mushroom and Leek Tart, 209

lemon
   Chia-Lemon Pots de Crème, 232
   Lemon Pistachio Loaf, 224
   Raspberry-Lemon Pancakes, 81

lentils
   Asparagus–Pearl Barley Risotto, 166
   Coconut Spinach Lentils, 192
   Crispy Pulses and Grains, 267
   Diversity Dal, 158
   Eggplant Parmigiana, 152
   Juno's Lasagna, 203
   Pearls and Puy, 265
   Pomegranate-Lentil Salad, 129
   Smashed Pea Bowl, 103
   Corn and Spinach Dal, 187

lettuce: Lima Bean Caesar, 126

lima beans
   Artichoke Lima Beans, 109
   Braised Beans and Greens, 196
   Lima Bean Caesar, 126
   Mushroom Stroganoff with Lima Bean Mash, 157
   Spicy Gochujang Beans, 87
   Whole Roast Cauliflower, 215
   Zucchini Lima Beans with Tomato Salsa, 171

"Meat" Balls, Black Bean, 180

Minestrone, 188

miso
   Always-There Risotto, 178
   Braised Beans and Greens, 196
   Juno's Lasagna, 203
   Kale and Cashew Soup, 113
   Kimchi Dressing, 270
   Miso Dressing, 270
   Miso-Spinach Eggs, 94
   Pea Soup with Crispy Caper Chickpeas, 184
   Tahini-Miso Beans, 106

Mixed ACV Pickles, 269
Mixed Berry Clafouti, 234
Mousse, Chocolate Olive Oil, 226
mozzarella: Eggplant Parmigiana, 152

mushrooms
   Always-There Risotto, 178
   Harissa-Hazelnut Roast, 212
   Harissa Mushrooms Seeded Bruschetta, 120
   Juno's Lasagna, 203
   Kale and Mushroom Salad, 149
   Mushroom and Leek Tart, 209
   Mushroom Stroganoff with Lima Bean Mash, 157
   Spicy Gochujang Beans, 87

navy beans
   11-Plant Orzo, 163
   Braised Beans and Greens, 196

noodles
   Eggplant Noodle Salad, 132
   Instant Noodles, 116

nuts
   Cinnamon-Pecan Granola, 70
   Curry Cashews, 253
   Hazelnut Gremolata–Corn Salad, 104
   Nut-and-Seed Loaf, 73
   Nut Crumb, 262
   Recharge Bars, 244
   Red Pepper–Quinoa Salad, 136

Seeded Soda Bread, 68
Sticky Maple and Cinnamon Nut Clusters, 252
Sweet and Savory Nuts, 252–3
Tim's Break-fast Bowl, 76

oat bran
Cinnamon-Pecan Granola, 70
Spiced Pear Oatmeal, 92

Oatmeal, Spiced Pear, 92

oats
Probiotic Bircher Muesli, 88
Spiced Pear Oatmeal, 92

olives
11-Plant Orzo, 163
Artichoke and Sun-Dried Tomato Stew, 191
Prebiotic Greek Salad, 145
Sheet-Pan Artichoke and Olive Bake, 160

orange: Carrot Cake with Tahini Orange Frosting, 230

Orzo, 11-Plant, 163

Palak Tofu, 169

pancakes
Herby Green-Pea Pancakes, 78
Raspberry-Lemon Pancakes, 81

Parmesan
Always-There Risotto, 178
Asparagus–Pearl Barley Risotto, 166
Braised Beans and Greens, 196
Cacio e Pepe Chickpeas, 108
Eggplant Parmigiana, 152

Parmigiana, Eggplant, 152

pasta
11-Plant Orzo, 163
Anchovy and Artichoke Pasta, 195
Broccolini and Walnut Orecchiette, 174
Creamy Kale Pasta, 100
Juno's Lasagna, 203
Minestrone, 188

pearl barley
Always-There Risotto, 178
Asparagus–Pearl Barley Risotto, 166
Crispy Pulses and Grains, 267
Pearls and Puy, 265

Pearls and Puy, 265

pears: Spiced Pear Oatmeal, 92

peas
Anchovy and Artichoke Pasta, 195
Braised Beans and Greens, 196
Greens and Beans Salad, 134
Herby Green-Pea Pancakes, 78
Mushroom and Leek Tart, 209
Pea Soup with Crispy Caper Chickpeas, 184
Red Pepper–Quinoa Salad, 136
Smashed Pea Bowl, 103
Whole Roast Cauliflower, 215

pecans
Apple Pecan Strudel, 237
Cinnamon-Pecan Granola, 70
Dark Chocolate Bark, 258
Pecan Chocolate Cookies, 221
Sticky Maple and Cinnamon Nut Clusters, 252

pecorino: Cacio e Pepe Chickpeas, 108

peppers
11-Plant Orzo, 163
Bulgur Bowl, 146
Bulgur with Aioli, 216
Instant Noodles, 116
Red Pepper–Quinoa Salad, 136
Sauerkraut Dressing, 271
Sauerkraut Frittata, 91
Sheet-Pan Roasted Eggplant, 200
Spinach Wraps with Roasted Pepper, 114

Pickles, Mixed ACV, 269

pistachios
Carrot and Fennel Salad with Halloumi, 142
Dark Chocolate Bark, 258
Lemon Pistachio Loaf, 224
Recharge Bars, 244
Whole Roast Cauliflower, 215

Polyphenol Salad, 141

pomegranate
Pomegranate-Lentil Salad, 129
Pomegranate Tabbouleh, 138

Prebiotic Greek Salad, 145
Probiotic Bircher Muesli, 88

quinoa
Diversity Dal, 158
Red Pepper–Quinoa Salad, 136

radicchio: Polyphenol Salad, 141
radishes: Instant Noodles, 116
raspberries, 81
Raspberry-Granola Crumble, 238
Raspberry-Lemon Pancakes, 81

Recharge Bars, 244

Red Pepper–Quinoa Salad, 136
risotto
  Always-There Risotto, 178
  Asparagus–Pearl Barley Risotto, 166
Roasted Broccolini–Tahini Salad, 130
Roasted Squash with Toasted Grains, 204

salads, 120
  Bulgur Bowl, 146
  Carrot and Fennel Salad with Halloumi, 142
  Eggplant Noodle Salad, 132
  Greens and Beans Salad, 134
  Hazelnut Gremolata–Corn Salad, 104
  Kale and Mushroom Salad, 149
  Lima Bean Caesar, 126
  Polyphenol Salad, 141
  Pomegranate-Lentil Salad, 129
  Pomegranate Tabbouleh, 138
  Prebiotic Greek Salad, 145
  Red Pepper–Quinoa Salad, 136
  Roasted Broccolini–Tahini Salad, 130
Sandwich, Green Goddess Chickpea, 110
sauerkraut
  Kale and Mushroom Salad, 149
  Red Pepper–Quinoa Salad, 136
  Sauerkraut, 64
  Sauerkraut Dressing, 271
  Sauerkraut Frittata, 91
  Spinach Wraps with Roasted Pepper, 114
Savory Crispy Pulses and Grains, 267
Schnitzel, Eggplant, 164
seeds
  Beet Hummus with Seeded Crackers, 246
  Chia-Lemon Pots de Crème, 232
  Cinnamon-Pecan Granola, 70
  Dark Chocolate Bark, 258
  Greens and Beans Salad, 134
  Nut-and-Seed Loaf, 73
  Pomegranate-Lentil Salad, 129
  Recharge Bars, 244
  Seed Mix Sprinkle, 263
  Seeded Bruschetta Three Ways, 120
  Seeded Soda Bread, 68
  Soy-Roasted Seeds, 254
  Tim's Break-fast Bowl, 76
Shakshuka, Green, 82
sheet-pan bakes
  Artichoke and Olive, 160
  Sheet-Pan Harissa Cabbage, 172
  Sheet-Pan Roasted Eggplant, 200

Sheet-Pan Roasted Eggplant, 200
Simple Kimchi, 67
Smashed Pea Bowl, 103
snow peas: Cashew-Cream Green Curry, 154
Soda Bread, Seeded, 68
soup
  Kale and Cashew Soup, 113
  Minestrone, 188
  Pea Soup with Crispy Caper Chickpeas, 184
Soy-Roasted Seeds, 254
Spiced Pear Oatmeal, 92
Spicy Gochujang Beans, 87
spinach
  Always-There Risotto, 178
  Braised Beans and Greens, 196
  Coconut Spinach Lentils, 192
  Corn Fritters, 96
  Corn and Spinach Dal, 187
  Diversity Dal, 158
  Miso-Spinach Eggs, 94
  Mushroom Stroganoff with Lima Bean Mash, 157
  Palak Tofu, 169
  Spicy Gochujang Beans, 87
  Spinach Wraps with Roasted Pepper, 114
split peas: Diversity Dal, 158
squash
  Diversity Dal, 158
  Roasted Squash with Toasted Grains, 204
Stew, Artichoke and Sun-Dried Tomato, 191
Sticky Maple and Cinnamon Nut Clusters, 252
Stroganoff, Mushroom with Lima Bean Mash, 157
Strudel, Apple Pecan, 237
Sweet and Savory Nuts, 252–3
Sweet Crispy Pulses and Grains, 267

Tabbouleh, Pomegranate, 138
tahini
  Carrot and Fennel Salad with Halloumi, 142
  Carrot Cake with Tahini Orange Frosting, 230
  Kale and Mushroom Salad, 149
  Miso Dressing, 270
  Roasted Broccolini–Tahini Salad, 130
  Roasted Squash with Toasted Grains, 204
  Sheet-Pan Roasted Eggplant, 200
  Tahini-Miso Beans, 106
Tart, Mushroom and Leek, 209

Tempeh Crumble, 266
Tim's Break-fast Bowl, 76
tofu
    Berry "Nice" Cream, 240
    Bulgur with Aioli, 216
    Chia-Lemon Pots de Crème, 232
    Corn Fritters, 96
    Eggplant Noodle Salad, 132
    Juno's Lasagna, 203
    Kimchi Dressing, 270
    Palak Tofu, 169

tomatoes
    11-Plant Orzo, 163
    Artichoke and Sun-Dried Tomato Stew, 191
    Black Bean Chili, 210
    Black Bean "Meat" Balls, 180
    Broccolini and Walnut Orecchiette, 174
    Corn Fritters, 96
    Eggplant Parmigiana, 152
    Juno's Lasagna, 203
    Minestrone, 188
    Palak Tofu, 169
    Pomegranate-Lentil Salad, 129
    Pomegranate Tabbouleh, 138
    Prebiotic Greek Salad, 145
    Roasted Broccolini–Tahini Salad, 130
    Sheet-Pan Harissa Cabbage, 172
    Sheet-Pan Roasted Eggplant Bake, 200
    Smashed Pea Bowl, 103
    Spicy Gochujang Beans, 87
    Tricolore Seeded Bruschetta, 122
    Zucchini Lima Beans with Tomato Salsa, 171

Tricolore Seeded Bruschetta, 122

walnuts
    Black Bean "Meat" Balls, 180
    Broccolini and Walnut Orecchiette, 174
    Mushroom and Leek Tart, 209
    Recharge Bars, 244
    Sticky Maple and Cinnamon Nut Clusters, 252

Whole Roast Cauliflower, 215
Wraps, Spinach with Roasted Pepper, 114

yogurt
    Harissa-Hazelnut Roast, 212
    Probiotic Bircher Muesli, 88
    Roasted Broccolini–Tahini Salad, 130
    Tim's Break-fast Bowl, 76

Zucchini
    11-Plant Orzo, 163
    Bulgur Bowl, 146
    Lemon Pistachio Loaf, 224
    Sheet-Pan Artichoke and Olive Bake, 160
    Zucchini Lima Beans with Tomato Salsa, 171
    Zucchini Flatbread, 248

General index

aging, 55
Amati, Federica, 11
amino acids, 24
anthocyanins, 19
antibiotics, 21
antioxidants, 21
autoimmune diseases, 15

bacteria, 14, 35, 42
beans *see* legumes
beta-carotene, 15, 57
Big IF Study, The, 42
bloating, 44
blood sugar levels, 54, 55
Blue Zones, 17, 199
bowel cancer, 16
brain function, 16
breakfast, 75

cadmium, 21
cancer, 16, 21, 55, 57
canned foods, 48, 172
carotenoids, 19
chocolate, 219
circadian rhythms, 41–2, 44, 75
climate change, 25–6
coffee, 16
color of vegetables *see* "Eat the Rainbow"
constipation, 44
Covid-19, 10
curry spices, 253

dairy farming, 26, 36
diabetes, 26, 55

"Eat the Rainbow," 19–23
extra-virgin olive oil, 52

fast eaters, 41
fermented foods, 16, 36–7, 41, 59
fertilizers, 21
fiber, 24, 27, 48, 55
fish/fishing, 26, 57
5:2 diet plan, 43
"five a day," 15–16, 18
flavonoids, 19
"flexitarian," 31
food allergies, 9
"Food for Life" principles, 45

frozen food, 53
full-fat foods, 54–5

growth hormones, 21
gut microbiome, 9, 13–17, 19, 34–5, 41–2, 44, 57, 75

H. Pylori bacteria, 9
Hadjigeorgiou, George, 10
"health halos," 33
heart disease, 9, 17, 26, 32, 57
herbs, 17–18, 177

inflammation, 9
intermittent fasting (IF) *see* time-restricted eating (TRE)
isoflavones, 57

juices and smoothies, 55

kefir, 35–7, 40
kimchi, 35, 36, 37
kombucha, 36, 40

lactose intolerance, 36
Lawsonibacter, 16
legumes, 15, 24–6, 31, 52–3, 57
low-fat foods, 54–5
lycopene, 57

meal times, 53–4
meat consumption, 25–6, 48–9, 55, 57, 151
meat substitutes, 31
Mediterranean diet, 17
mental health disorders, 31, 32
metabolic diseases, 32
mirepoix, 17, 177
Monteiro, Carlo, 32

National Food Strategy, UK, 32
neurological problems, 21
NOVA classification system, 32, 34
nuts and seeds, 17–18, 57

obesity, 9, 26, 55
organic foods, 21–2, 53
overnight fasting *see* time-restricted eating (TRE)

peeling fruit and vegetables, 53
pesticides, 21–2, 53
phytochemicals, 15–17, 26
phytoestrogen, 57

plant-based protein, 25–6, 30
polyphenols, 14, 19, 21, 22–23, 48, 53
potassium, 58
pregnancy, 42
probiotics, 16
processed foods, 31
processed meats, 55
protein, 24–7, 30–31, 57
pulses, 15, 18, 26, 50, 52

raw vegetables, 57

salt, 58
saturated fat, 55
sauerkraut, 36–7, 40
"Singapore trial," 17
slow eaters, 41
snacks, 33, 243
social eating, 199
soybeans, 57
spices, 17–18
sugar, 219
sulforaphane, 15

tea, 16
"30 plants" diet, 13–17, 23, 48, 52, 125
time-restricted eating (TRE), 41–4, 59
tooth decay, 55
TwinsUK, 36
Tyler, Georgia, 11

ultra-processed foods (UPFs), 21, 26, 31–5, 99

vegans, 27, 30, 49, 58
vegetarians, 25
vinegar, 54
vitamins, 15

washing fruit and vegetables, 53
Wolf, Jonathan, 10
World Health Organization, 26

yogurt, 35–37

ZOE, 10–11, 14, 16, 18, 27, 30, 36, 41, 42, 48
ZOE Score, 48

References

For sources and references relating to the introduction of this cookbook, please scan:

Acknowledgments

More than any other book I have written, this cookbook has been a major team effort. In my ignorance, I had no clue it would be so complex, and I have learned so much from working with this brilliant group of professionals to create it. Alongside my amazing publisher at Penguin Random House, Bea Hemming, I've been working with Jenny Dean for the past year, who, recognizing the success of *Food for Life*, persuaded me that this cookbook was needed. Jenny was our ringmaster and also coordinated the pieces of a constantly shifting puzzle, keeping us all on time. My literary and media agents, Sophie Lambert and Vanessa Fogarty, provided encouragement and support, as always.

It was immediately clear that we should join forces with the expert team at ZOE to create this cookbook. Jonathan Wolf, my ZOE cofounder and friend, instantly shared my vision to bring the theory behind ZOE into practice through a book of accessible recipes with the potential to help people improve their health in their own homes. Summarizing the science of healthy eating behind the recipes was my job, helped immensely by ZOE's head nutritionist, Dr. Federica Amati, and Marie Ellis, who improved it and corrected most of my mistakes.

Georgia Tyler is the mastermind behind ZOE's Instagram and the hugely popular recipes that appear on it. The book features some of our community's favorite recipes from ZOE's Instagram alongside new recipes created by Kathryn Bruton, who also brought all the recipes together in the form you find them here. I want to especially thank all the nutrition coaches and support staff at ZOE who enthusiastically tested all our recipes in their spare time, gave vital feedback, and checked the scores. The most fun part for me was going to the photo shoot, where all I had to do was eat and be surrounded by lovely people and delicious food—what a job. . . .

Crucial to the book's creation were Josh Williams, Issy Croker, and Emily Ezekiel, who made the food and book look beautiful. I'm grateful to Clare Sayer, Caroline Stearns, and Graeme Hall for the accuracy of their eyes. To the wider team at Vintage, led by Hannah Telfer and including Alison Davies and Katrina Northern for the campaign, Jamie Taylor in production, and Nat Breakwell and everyone in the sales team, thank you. Lastly, I'm grateful to the whole amazing team at ZOE who pulled together to make this happen and especially to Sharon Feder, Mary Rochester Gearing, Vlad Zely, and Rhea D'Souza. There are many more to thank than can be listed here. To everyone who has been involved, thank you.

Tim Spector, MD, is professor of epidemiology at King's College London. He is the bestselling author of *The Diet Myth*, *Spoon-Fed*, and *Food for Life*, and scientific cofounder of ZOE, the nutrition science company. With a focus on cutting-edge science and honored with an OBE for his impactful work in fighting Covid-19, Tim stands at the forefront of his field. The original pioneer of microbiome research, he is among the top 100 most cited scientists in the world.

ZOE is a science and nutrition company on a mission to improve the health of millions. Through resources like social media, their chart-topping podcast, and this book, ZOE supports people to make smarter food choices so they can feel better and have more years of good health. Individual food scores are revealed with ZOE membership, which combines results from at-home testing with world-leading science to help you find meal combinations and ways of eating that work for your body. Find out more and sign up at www.zoe.com.

Ten Speed Press
An imprint of the Crown Publishing Group
A division of Penguin Random House LLC
1745 Broadway
New York, NY, 10019
tenspeed.com
penguinrandomhouse.com

Introduction copyright © 2025 by Tim Spector.
Recipes copyright © 2025 by ZOE.

Penguin Random House values and supports copyright. Copyright fuels creativity, encourages diverse voices, promotes free speech, and creates a vibrant culture. Thank you for buying an authorized edition of this book and for complying with copyright laws by not reproducing, scanning, or distributing any part of it in any form without permission. You are supporting writers and allowing Penguin Random House to continue to publish books for every reader. Please note that no part of this book may be used or reproduced in any manner for the purpose of training artificial intelligence technologies or systems.

Ten Speed Press and the Ten Speed Press colophon are registered trademarks of Penguin Random House LLC.

Originally published in hardcover in Great Britain by Jonathan Cape, an imprint of Vintage, a division of Penguin Random House UK, London, in 2024.

Typeface: Latinotype's Boston

Library of Congress Control Number: 2024951371

Hardcover ISBN 978-0-593-83863-1
Ebook ISBN 978-0-593-83864-8

Editor: Kelly Snowden | Production editor: Abby Oladipo | Editorial assistant: Gabby Urena Matos
Designer: Josh Williams | Design manager: Kelly Booth
Production designers: Mari Gill and Faith Hague
Production manager: Jane Chinn
Food and prop stylist: Emily Ezekiel
Recipe developers: Kathryn Bruton and Georgia Tyler
Photographer: Issy Croker | Illustrator: Josh Williams
Proofreaders: Clancy Brown, Heather Rodino, Lorie Young, Sigi Nacson, Penelope Haynes, and Carla Jablonski
Publicists: Jana Branson and Jina Stanfill
Marketers: Brianne Sperber and Allison Renzulli

Manufactured in China

10 9 8 7 6 5 4 3 2 1

First US Edition

The authorized representative in the EU for product safety and compliance is Penguin Random House Ireland, Morrison Chambers, 32 Nassau Street, Dublin D02 YH68, Ireland, https://eu-contact.penguin.ie.